IDENTITY, DEVELOPMENT, AND THE POLITICS OF THE PAST

T0308905

IDENTITY, DEVELOPMENT, AND THE POLITICS OF THE PAST

*An Ethnography of Continuity and Change
in a Coastal Ecuadorian Community*

D A N I E L   B A U E R

UNIVERSITY PRESS OF COLORADO
Louisville

Published by University Press of Colorado
245 Century Circle, Suite 202
Louisville, Colorado 80027

The University Press of Colorado is a proud member of the Association of University Presses.

The University Press of Colorado is a cooperative publishing enterprise supported, in part, by Adams State University, Colorado State University, Fort Lewis College, Metropolitan State University of Denver, Regis University, University of Colorado, University of Northern Colorado, Utah State University, and Western State Colorado University.

∞ This paper meets the requirements of the ANSI/NISO Z39.48-1992 (Permanence of Paper).

ISBN: 978-1-60732-759-2 (cloth)
ISBN: 978-1-60732-819-3 (paper)
ISBN: 978-1-60732-760-8 (ebook)
DOI: https://doi.org/10.5876/9781607327608

Library of Congress Cataloging-in-Publication Data

Names: Bauer, Daniel, 1977– author.
Title: Identity, development, and the politics of the past : an ethnography of continuity and change in a coastal Ecuadorian community / Daniel Bauer.
Description: Boulder : University Press of Colorado, [2018] | Includes bibliographical references and index.
Identifiers: LCCN 2018017669| ISBN 9781607327592 (cloth) | | ISBN 9781607328193 (pbk) ISBN 9781607327608 (ebook)
Subjects: LCSH: Ecuadorians—Ethnic identity. | Salango (Ecuador)—Social conditions. | Salango (Ecuador)—Economic conditions. | Ecuador—Ethnic relations. | Ecuador—Politics and government. | Bauer, Daniel, 1977–
Classification: LCC F3791.S23 B38 2018 | DDC 305.8009866—dc23
LC record available at https://lccn.loc.gov/2018017669

Cover illustration: "Los Balseros" by Cristina Guillén, used with permission.

To the residents of Salango

Contents

Figures

Acknowledgments

I am grateful to many people and institutions that provided support for my research and for the writing of this project. I am most indebted to the people of Salango and especially to the Gutiérrez-Guillén family for making this project possible and for having a profound impact on my life.

I recognize that published works are not the result of only the work of the author. Numerous individuals contribute to the final product, whether through encouragement to continue writing, reading various drafts of chapters, providing support in the field, suggesting additional literature to read, helping with edits, fielding questions about where to publish, or patiently listening to complaints and frustrations. For these things I owe a debt of gratitude to various individuals who provided me with guidance and support over the years.

Michael Harris and Valentina Martínez introduced me to Ecuador and provided me with the opportunity to work in Salango. I am grateful for their longstanding support of my research. Jonathan Hill, Emma Cervone, Andy Hofling, and Jane Adams worked with me through the dissertation stages of this project (Bauer 2008) and have been influential in helping me gain perspective and move forward in my research. I also owe a great deal of thanks to David Kozak and Tony Webster for listening to my questions and providing feedback throughout the publication process. Each of these people was instrumental in the research and writing of this book, and I am extremely grateful to all of them.

I wish to acknowledge multiple people who reviewed all or portions of this project in its various stages. In all cases, peer reviews helped improve the quality of research and the writing in every chapter of this book. I am especially grateful to Lucas Savino and Geoff Read for helping me think more critically about plurinationalism as related to my work. I also want to make special mention of the peer reviewers for the University Press of Colorado. Their knowledge of the themes covered in this book and their constructive feedback improved the quality of the finished product. I have no doubts that this book is stronger as a result of their input.

I am very thankful for the support of Anna Stroulia, who took time out of her busy schedule to review each chapter in a timely manner and provide critical insights and feedback. I also thank Jessica Keller for reviewing each chapter and for helping me compile the glossary.

Multiple institutions provided critical funding and opportunities for fieldwork. I am extremely grateful to Florida Atlantic University, Southern Illinois University–Carbondale, and the University of Southern Indiana. Florida Atlantic University provided me with financial support for the early stages of my research, and it was through a Dissertation Research Award funded by Southern Illinois University–Carbondale that I was able to complete the bulk of my dissertation research. The University of Southern Indiana Foundation provided funding for multiple postdoctoral research trips. This book would not be possible without the generosity of each of these institutions.

The editorial staff at the University Press of Colorado worked in a dedicated manner to make this book a reality. I want to make special acknowledgment of Jessica d'Arbonne. Jessica worked with me from the beginning stages of this project with the University Press of Colorado, and she was always considerate of my needs and timely in her responses to my queries. Working with Jessica was a pleasure. I am also grateful to Laura Furney, Cheryl Carnahan, Beth Svinarich, Dan Pratt, and many other individuals who contributed to the project.

I acknowledge and thank the following for permission to use material I published previously: Wiley-Blackwell, the *Bulletin of Latin American Research*, *The Applied Anthropologist*, and *La Revista de Antropólogia Experimental*.

I am grateful to my family and especially to my wife, Viviana, for providing me with much needed encouragement to continue to move forward with this project.

A crowd gathered on the beach as the sun set just past the island. The water glistened with reds, oranges, and yellows as the surf rolled slowly to the shore. It was 1524, and a raft was setting sail from the village of Salango for a long-distance trading expedition. As the raft lumbered past the island toward the open ocean to the west, the sail was barely visible through the penetrating light of the setting sun. Water surged over the deck of the raft, and the ocean churned beneath as a result of various rocky outcrops and a convergence of multiple currents. The logs creaked and moaned under the weight of tons of cargo, with the raft rising quickly and dropping suddenly as waves passed. This was likely the occurrence on many evenings as rafts left the beach of Salango in the early 1500s. However, in 1525 things changed. Spanish colonizers encountered a raft off the coast of Salango, and things would never be the same. The chronicles recorded by the Spanish tell of a people from a place known as Calangane and a raft that carried precious shells, beads, textiles, pots, silver, gold, and emeralds (Murra 1963). The people would come to be known as the Manta. Following colonial conquest, genocide, and assimilation in the late 1500s and early 1600s, Ecuadorian independence in 1809, commercial agricultural production in the early 1900s, and the emergence of a commercial fishing industry in the 1970s, life in the village would bear little resemblance to what it had been shortly after the conquest of the Americas.

DOI: 10.5876/9781607327608.c000

For most visitors to Salango, it is an off-the-beaten-path community on the Ecuadorian coast that, while typical of the coastal fishing culture of rural Manabí province, does not overtly reflect anything that would suggest an Indigenous identity or a strong connection to the past. People gather at the beach and the sun reflects off the water as multi-ton diesel-powered fishing boats leave the bay most evenings to fish the waters off the coast. The same path is followed beyond the island and into the depths. Spanish is the only language spoken, aside from a few individuals who also comprehend English but do not necessarily speak the language. No Indigenous language is spoken.[1] Bicycles and pickup trucks cruise the dusty streets; cell phones, satellite dishes, and the internet are increasingly common.

Despite the contemporary situation, Salango has been the focus of archaeologists since initial excavations in the region in the 1970s; it is not an exaggeration to suggest that Salango is well-known, if not famous, within the sphere of Andean archaeology. I have at times felt rather uncomfortable with this fact. As an ethnographer, I was always taught to protect the identity of those I work with and to use pseudonyms not only for individuals but also for communities. However, as my work intersects with concerns that are archaeological in nature, I find this a difficult, if not problematic, proposal. Thus, I have decided not to use pseudonyms for communities mentioned in this book. I struggled with this decision, but I think it will do justice to the legacy of Salango as well as other communities; ultimately, a wealth of published data and sources pertaining to the community and the region are relevant for understanding what is forthcoming in this volume. Evidence from excavations and surveys conducted throughout the region support the existence of a community that was part of the far-reaching expanses of the Inca empire and that participated in the long-distance trade reported by the Spanish. Even as the goal of most archaeological research in the area is to support a variety of claims about regional growth, trade networks, political expansion, and cosmology, there is a need to focus on Salango as a contemporary community in coastal Ecuador and, more important, on how Salango's past influences the present.

Today, Salango is a village defined by a commercial fishing industry, a connection to global tourism, native-born residents who live abroad, the presence of numerous national and international researchers, and local political institutions that draw on the past to assert claims to identity in the present. This book is about Salango's present and its connections to the past. In what follows, I attempt to link the past and present to answer questions about the Salango of today. I want the record of Salango not to be limited only to what is known about the prehistory of the region. As such, this book is concerned with peoples' understandings of the past and with how the past influences development (changes) in the present. It is my hope that this book will be a short chapter in the extensive history of Salango.

NOTE

1. I use the capital "I" for Indigenous and the capital "N" for Native as an indicator of respect and to correspond to a growing trend by academics working with and writing about Indigenous peoples and cultures (see Becker 2008; Pierotti 2011; Yellow Bird 1999).

IDENTITY, DEVELOPMENT, AND
THE POLITICS OF THE PAST

I

Introduction

Into the Field

The sun beat down with intensity as I walked down the dirt street toward the recently opened internet café. The café was housed in the living room, or *sala*, of a small cement house connected to several other homes and painted in a faded white paint. In the previous ten years the home had seen numerous residents, some of whom I came to know well and others I only recognized by face and not by name. I entered, passing under an awning covered in palm thatch, and made my way into the shade where the temperature felt twenty degrees cooler. Five small computer stations were lined neatly along the wall, separated by flimsy plywood dividers. Youth in their early teens, most of whom I had known since they were toddlers, smiled and joked with one another while they played on the computers—young boys, their dark black hair slicked back or spiked high with hair gel, and young girls sitting close and giggling while sharing the same computer. This sight would not have existed four years earlier, at least not in this community. As I stood there, with the hope of checking my e-mail, I reflected momentarily on the changes that had taken place in Salango since my initial introduction to the community ten years earlier.

This is a book about change and continuity, the past and the present. It is concerned with life in a rural Ecuadorian fishing village and about understanding processes of culture change that impact the daily lives of residents. This book is about the economies, identities,

DOI: 10.5876/9781607327608.c001

3

political struggles, development practices, and local-global interactions experienced by people living in a small ocean-side community. Based on my experiences with local residents, political activists, and agents of change, I argue that local conceptions of identity play a prominent role in shaping economic and political transitions in Salango. I endeavor to demonstrate how Salangueños, a group historically recognized as *mestizo* (of mixed European and Indigenous descent), make claims to an Indigenous identity by asserting a connection to the past through links to the archaeological record as well as processes of work that connect people to place. These intersecting themes provide Salangueños with a foundation on which claims to identity and a sense of belonging are constructed. Moreover, I suggest that ethnic identity in Salango is part of a complex matrix that includes economics, politics, history, and the archaeological record and that is influenced by forces that extend well beyond the boundaries of the community.

In the pages that follow, I detail my experiences living and conducting research in coastal Ecuador while focusing on the dynamic nature of ethnic identity. At a general level, I explore the relationship between identity and economic practice in coastal Ecuador while simultaneously looking at the ways ethnic identity, history, and economic practice influence development and how development practices can foster new understandings of ethnic identities. While the focus of this book is on the particular community of Salango, I make a concerted effort to illustrate how the community is linked to global processes that extend far beyond the boundaries of the village. I also recognize that no ethnography gives a complete picture of the cultural context, and all ethnographies are partial, both in the sense that they reflect the perspective of the ethnographer and also by providing an incomplete account of the culture under study (Clifford 1986). Thus, I do not claim that this ethnography is a comprehensive account of culture in Salango, but it does reflect, albeit in part, the experiences of Salangueños as well as my own experiences during a time of significant change in the community.

My interest in Latin America began with study abroad opportunities throughout high school and college and included trips to Costa Rica and Mexico that fostered my desire to expand my knowledge about culture in Latin America. I was drawn to contemporary culture as well as archaeology, and this interest expanded as I traveled to Mayan ruins and later spent time visiting villages in Amazonian Peru. My introduction to coastal Ecuador began under the auspices of a field program. Not unlike many early anthropologists, contemporary students are often introduced to the field by way of an adviser and mentor. My situation was no different, and I am extremely grateful for having had such an opportunity.

I first arrived in Ecuador in the summer of 2002. Despite my initial intention to conduct dissertation research in lowland Peru, I was quickly drawn to the Ecuadorian coast and its residents. Locals impressed me with their humility, work ethic, generosity, and sincerity. The initial six weeks I spent in the field proved valuable to introducing me to the local cultural context while affording me the opportunity to establish relationships that would influence my research in impactful and unanticipated ways. At the same time, my time spent in Ecuador would help shape me as an individual, an educator, and a scholar of Latin America.

It was late June 2002. While standing conspicuously in the middle of the street, I was greeted by a young man about my age. He waved me down from a distance as he stood inside what I was later told was his family's open-air restaurant. The restaurant consisted of a white painted wall extending about 1 meter up from ground level and a vast opening above that stretched to the beginnings of a large conical thatched roof. I looked in from a distance as my eyes adjusted to the change in light from the sun-penetrated street to the shadowed interior. He motioned multiple times by waving his arm in a manner that clearly indicated that he wanted me to come closer. I hesitated a bit and then made my way toward him.

With a somewhat perplexed look yet an inviting demeanor, he asked what I was doing. I responded that I was making a map, and he asked me to come inside and share it with him. I walked around the outside of the restaurant and into the entrance. The restaurant was humble but hospitable. The floors were cement, and a number of chairs and tables made of *caña* (bamboo) or local wood were arranged throughout. I began speaking with my inquisitor, whose name I would learn was Diego. His build was stocky and his features were slightly weathered beyond his age of twenty-four. He inquired about my backpack and water bottle. Diego informed me that he had recently returned from Venezuela where he had spent the previous couple of years working in the bustling capital city, Carácas. I could see in his eyes and hear in his voice that he was attempting to reestablish himself and make the transition from an urban experience in a foreign country to a return to his native community, a village he would later refer to as a place that does not exist on the map because of its decidedly rural characteristics and perceived remoteness and isolation. I left after a short time, without giving much thought to the fact that the brief conversation Diego and I shared would lead to a long-term friendship and a deep understanding of and respect for one another.

I left Salango in August of that year with a promise made to Diego and other friends and acquaintances that I would return, and I did so on numerous occasions over subsequent years. Each time I returned, throughout the course of my dissertation research and succeeding postdoctoral trips, I paid attention to the changes that were taking place in Salango. There was a familiarity during each trip but also a sense of profound newness brought forth by visible changes, such as the paving of the main road that leads into town and the construction of new homes, as well as abstract changes related to community politics and a transitioning economy.

FIELDWORK AND FRIENDSHIP

My initial foray into life in coastal Ecuador led to a longitudinal research project that included numerous trips back to the field on various occasions over more than a decade. In total, I spent approximately 30 months in the small community of Salango, with the majority of that time falling between the years 2006 and 2008. In my earliest research trips, I resided in the local archaeological museum known as CIMS (*Centro de Investigaciones Museo Salango*), and it was not until a set of unfortunate circumstances occurred that I was invited to reside with a local family. Through my experiences living with a family and the changes in my position from outsider to a known individual in the community, I was able to gain insights into life in an Ecuadorian fishing village. The fact that I traveled back and forth to Salango on no fewer than a dozen occasions also provided me with perspective throughout the duration of my research. Being at home for months at a time gave me the ability to pause and reflect on my research while also affording me the opportunity to formulate new research questions. This is something I do not feel I would have been able to accomplish if I had stayed in the field for a single period of time. However, being away from the field and then returning often left me with questions upon my return about things I had missed while I was away.

I arrived in Salango in May 2005 as part of my dissertation fieldwork, and I set up my room in one of the small wooden cabins in the museum compound near the beach. I unpacked some of my things as an evening breeze blew in from the nearby ocean. The smell of salt was thick in the air as the sun set to the west. Donald, an expat from the United States and a longtime administrator of the museum, invited me to meet with him and a fellow researcher for dinner at one of the two small restaurants in town. Donald was always happy to have someone to talk to and would often vent his frustrations about life in the village. He had spent nearly twenty years living in Salango, and his patience with local politics and life in the village often wore thin. We left the museum at about 6:00 p.m. and walked through the dimly lit streets.

We returned to the museum after a couple hours of conversation, and I walked through the darkness to my cabin at the edge of the museum compound. The compound extends along the riverbank on one side and is flanked by the main roadway that enters town on the other. There are a few homes nearby, but it is a solitary space that is covered in darkness at night because of large trees that block out much of the moonlight even on the brightest nights.

I had an uneasy feeling, as in the past I had experienced having items stolen when I had gone out in the evening. I walked slowly up the wooden steps and onto the front porch of the cabin. The air was dense, and the only sound was that of waves crashing against the shore. I faced the door and the window to the left that I had closed and locked from the inside before I went to dinner. Seeing that the door was closed, I reached up and pushed on the wooden shutters of the window. They opened. My heart sank, and my chest began pounding. Someone had managed to get into my cabin. I quickly unlocked the door and entered. At first inspection, everything appeared normal. Clothes were laid out tidily on the bed. Items were as I had left them when I had unpacked some things before going to dinner. I looked more closely and realized that my large duffle bag, which was only partially unpacked, was not tucked neatly below the bed where I had left it. It was gone. How did someone get in, I wondered. My eyes scanned the room. As I looked to the ceiling, I noticed that part of the bamboo wall had been broken away close to the point where it met the ceiling. I rushed outside and looked. My feet kicked up moist sand as I hustled around the side of the cabin. To my shock, there was a wooden ladder leading up to where the opening had been made. I realized then that the ladder, used for maintenance around the museum compound, had been previously under the elevated cabin. I ran to the office to notify Donald and told him I was going to head across town to tell Diego what had happened. My choice to tell Diego was based on our established friendship and the confidence I had built with him and his family.

I ran most of the 500 meters or so to the house of Diego's family. Diego and his mother, one sister, and three brothers were outside, Diego relaxing in a hammock and the rest of his family seated on plastic chairs and a crude wooden bench. "They robbed me," I said with a sense of urgency and desperation. Diego quickly asked "Who? What happened?" I tried my best to explain the situation in my state of distress. Diego and his brother Manuel, whom I had come to know quite well along with the rest of the family, agreed that we needed to call the police. Fortunately, the telephone was working. Service was and still is very unreliable, and at the time most houses in town did not have telephones. The police would have to come from the nearby town of Puerto

López and would probably arrive in twenty minutes or so. Diego, Manuel, and their brother Gustavo (referred to from here on as *los hermanos* [the brothers]), and I hurried back to the museum to wait for the police. The police said they would come back the next day to talk in more detail about what had happened. It was late and they seemed to have little interest in helping. The brothers decided that the best decision was for me to leave the museum and take up residence in a spare room in the upstairs of their parents' home.

The home of don Orlando and doña Luisa is humble. It is two stories and built of wood mixed with handmade brick. It is typical of an older home in Salango. The stairs leading to the second floor are narrow and steep, and, as they are today, they were heavily damaged as a result of termites. Care has to be taken not to step on any floor boards that are too soft to hold one's weight. Exposed electrical wires hang low where the stairs meet the second floor. The upstairs consists of two small rooms, divided by plywood walls with open doorways. At the time, the upstairs was not in use because of its poor condition and probably also because no children were living at home. Instead, it was more of a storage area, akin to an attic back home in the United States. The exception was a bed in one of the rooms that was covered in plastic sheeting to protect it from the pair of pigeons that had taken up residence in the rafters. It was dusty and unkempt, but it was safe. I went to bed that night feeling grateful for the support given to me by the family, although questions lingered in my mind as to how the burglary had happened and who was responsible for stealing my items.

I awoke in the middle of the night with terrible stomach pains. I scurried down the stairs and to the back of the house in desperate need of a bathroom. I had been in the house before but no further than the sala, so I did not know where to find the bathroom. I looked and looked, but no luck. There was only a small room at the back of the house with a cement basin for washing clothes. A doorway led to the backyard. No bathroom. The need was urgent. I ran outside in the darkness of night and over to the side door of the restaurant. It was unlocked. I knew there was a bathroom inside, and I quickly made it to my destination. The night continued with multiple trips up and down the stairs, in and out of the bathroom. When I awoke in the morning I was greeted by Diego and doña Luisa sitting outside. "Good morning . . . how did you sleep?" they asked, even though it was apparent that they knew I had suffered through a long night of intestinal discomfort. They likely also struggled to sleep as they heard me go up and down the stairs and in and out of the bathroom on no fewer than four occasions. I explained that I was a little under the weather, and they shared with me that until I felt better I would be sleeping in Diego's room in the restaurant, which had a private bathroom. Doña Luisa offered to prepare me *unas tostadas* (some toast) and *un aguita* (an herbal remedy) to improve my stomach problems.

As the result of a precarious sequence of circumstances, I was invited into a household, and years later I can say that I have been treated like a member of the family. I would later build a small room attached to Manuel's house that I would ultimately turn over to him as his young family grew. We would celebrate birthdays, mourn deaths, and welcome new members into the family. At times we would argue, but more often we would agree. I have come to consider doña Luisa a second mother and Diego, Manuel, and all of their siblings brothers and sisters of my own, and they frequently refer to me as *un otro hermano* (another brother). I am the *padrino* (godfather) to Manuel's children as well as to the oldest son of his brother Gustavo. We share a close relationship of camaraderie and confidence despite our differences. Diego and Manuel are the youngest of nine siblings. They grew up in a rural Ecuadorian fishing village, where their childhood was spent living in a house made of bamboo. They both worked as fishermen and divers, and their work took them from the Ecuadorian coast to the Galapagos Islands. I, in contrast, am one of two siblings, and I was raised in Illinois in a small suburb of Chicago. I grew up on a gentleman's farm, and my formative years were spent doing daily chores, including caring for pigs, geese, goats, and horses and baling hay in the summer.

Beyond our cultural differences, one thing that undoubtedly framed my experiences in Salango is the fact that I am a white male. To locals, I am a *gringo*.[1] I am light skinned and light eyed, and in many ways I am viewed as somewhat exotic. This is not to say that residents of Salango have not had significant contact with outsiders, but they do note difference, and that difference carries meaning that shapes relationships and influences interactions. Would I have been invited into the home of doña Luisa and given Diego's room if it were not for my background as a white American? I am not so sure. If I were not a gringo, would other Ecuadorians who visited the family restaurant inquire about me while enjoying a meal? Would I have been freely accepted as a tagalong guest at birthday parties, graduation celebrations, and other events that are normally reserved for close friends and family members? Would I have been asked to provide financial support to help local schools in the area that were understaffed? Would I have been asked to judge local beauty pageants, as I was on numerous occasions? I suspect that in all these cases I would have been treated differently if it were not for my race and nationality. As such, I recognize that I was accepted in part because of how I was perceived by local residents. I was not viewed as a threat, and in some ways locals viewed forming relationships with me as advantageous as they attempted to build social capital.

Residents also positioned me with respect to their previous interactions with gringos, including researchers, ex-pats, and Peace Corps volunteers. The point is that race matters in Ecuador, and it most certainly impacted my research and how I understand the experiences I had in Salango. As a gringo, I did not carry the baggage associated with colonialism, and I stood outside the ethno-racial matrix that is prominent in Ecuadorian society. I would be cued into this reality on numerous occasions when locals were far more reticent to interact with Ecuadorian "outsiders" who represented ethnic, racial, and class differences than they were to interact with me. In times where interactions between local residents and Ecuadorian outsiders did occur, the tensions associated with status and difference were often present. In contrast, I was often treated with caution and care, not unlike the way a parent might treat a child. Friends and acquaintances were quick to look after me and to make sure I was safe and well-fed. This points not only to the warm and giving nature of Salangueños but also to the fact that I was an outsider (a gringo), and for that I was treated with a degree of difference.

Through my friendship with los hermanos, I gained perspective as to what it means to live life in a rural Ecuadorian village. By participating in daily activities, community events, the labor of fishing, and the joys and struggles of daily life, the themes of development, identity, continuity, and change emerged as foci of my research. This book is the story of that research. To protect the identity and respect the privacy of my consultants and friends, I use pseudonyms throughout this book when referring to individuals. The only exceptions are don Orlando, whose song is presented in chapter 2, and certain public figures.

I sat with Manuel while a karate action film played on the television screen at the front of the bus. It was one of the numerous films that are poorly made and too frequently shown on the bumpy ride from Guayaquil to the Manabí coast. The star of the film looked familiar. It was Dolph Lundgren, the actor who played the Russian boxer in *Rocky IV* and who has achieved a recent resurgence in Hollywood action films. Manuel focused little attention on the film and instead rested his eyes in the comfort of the air-conditioned bus. The combination of air conditioning and a movie seems to do the trick to induce sleep. I recall my second trip to Ecuador when Manuel, Diego, and three other friends met me in Guayaquil, Ecuador's largest city and an industrial port about four hours south of Salango. I invited them to the movies, a treat for them considering that they only made trips to the city perhaps once a year and most of them had only been to a movie once in their lives. I looked around about fifteen minutes into the film and noticed that they were all asleep in their chairs.

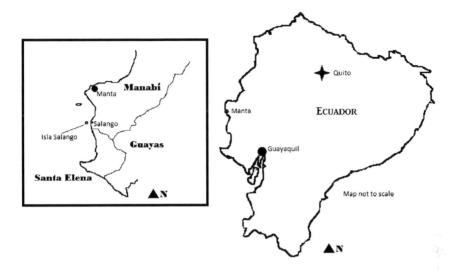

FIGURE I.I. *Map of study region*

The ride to Salango out of the urban sprawl of Guayaquil is winding and bumpy, and it travels through agricultural land that produces rice, cacao, and bananas to the lush hills of Manabí province. As one moves closer to the Manabí coast, traffic decreases and the road is dominated by commercial trucks carrying agricultural goods and the ever-present buses loaded with passengers who use Ecuador's efficient public transportation system as the main means of moving from town to town and province to province. The gears of the large diesel buses grind as drivers push the speed to make it to the next stop in a timely fashion. The main line stops in the bustling city of Jipijapa, where the intense sun bakes the streets as dust blows in the air. Jipijapa was once known as the center of Ecuadorian coffee production, but production declined in the 1990s and most of the downtown warehouses closed. Today, the city is predominantly a transition point for travelers who switch from the inter-provincial bus line to one of the many local lines that provide service south from Jipijapa to the province of Santa Elena and north to cities, including the provincial capital of Portoviejo and the lively port city of Manta.

Manuel woke up. "*Vamos, Styk*" (Let's go, Styk). Manuel assigned to me the *apodo* (nickname) Styk a number of years ago. I do not know why Manuel decided to give me that nickname, but it has stuck and is now what he uses to refer to me on virtually all occasions. Nicknames are so commonplace in coastal Ecuador that almost everyone has one, and sometimes even distant cousins only know each other by their nicknames. I was once told the story of three friends who were returning to the village after spending some time in Guayaquil. One of the friends spoke to his mother in the village shortly before getting on the bus in Guayaquil and relayed that he was traveling with *Fiebre* (fever) and *Paludismo* (malaria). The mother did not realize that Fiebre and Paludismo were the apodos of her son's traveling companions, and she urged her son not to travel if he was ill.

We scrambled to get off the bus and grab my bags. We made our way inside the terminal, followed by a quick turn toward the restroom. A small fee must be paid to an attendant sitting at a rickety table just outside the bathroom. The amount depends on the reason for your visit. The bathroom is dank and sticky. There is no running water, and the chance of having sufficient toilet paper is wholly dependent on your ability to convince the attendant to give you more than the standard three squares that come with the entrance fee. Despite this disparaging review, I cannot help but smile when I think of how this compares to the simple things that are taken for granted in public restrooms in the United States. In fact, there is something stimulating about the makings of life in rural Ecuador, even when life means making a visit to the restroom at the bus terminal in Jipijapa.

Our next stop was outside the terminal. The area is almost always bustling. Dust and diesel fumes fill the air; the organic sounds of conversations, calls, and laughter intermingle with the mechanical sounds of revving engines, squealing brakes, and automobile and bus horns. Vendors move about selling everything from candies to cigarettes to ready-to-eat *arroz con pollo* (chicken with rice), and the terminal is one of the only places to purchase coffee beans despite the prominent history of coffee production in Jipijapa and the surrounding region. I have a couple of things that I always purchase when making a stop in Jipijapa. We ordered two cups of coffee and two one-pound bags of ground beans. The coffee is dark, hot, and sweet. It invigorated us as we stretched our legs before the next leg of our journey. Next up was a loaf of banana bread. The gentleman who sells the bread appears to be in his fifties. He is slender and well dressed, always wearing a shirt, slacks, and tie with a gold cross suspended from a long gold chain that hangs around his neck. The bread was warm to the touch and wrapped in brown paper, then tucked snugly into a transparent plastic bag. I purchased a single loaf for Manuel and me to split. We were approached by another gentleman who carried a large, round plastic tub with oranges neatly stacked inside. I encounter him every time I pass through Jipijapa. In broken English he asked, "You from New York? You go to Montañita, my friend?" Montañita is a well-known gringo enclave and surf/party town located on the southern coast. I politely told him "no, I am going to Manabí," as I do every time. We engaged in casual conversation for a few moments before Manuel tapped me on the arm and pointed to the waiting bus.

The terminal of Jipijapa reflects salient features of regional culture, and a great deal can be gleaned from spending time there. The informal economy is alive and well. Cash is the currency, and local cuisine echoes the importance of agriculture and fishing throughout the region. The local cheese is sold fresh by merchants who have small stands, and vendors move about offering ready-to-eat meals that range from the mainstream *bolones* (balls of fried plantain mixed with cheese or pork) to more exotic dishes like *corviche* (fish wrapped and cooked in plantain dough that is deep fried) and *fritadas* (seasoned and fried pork pieces). Food is prepared in nearby homes and brought fresh to the terminal, where it is sold in plastic containers or bags. The same vendors, both children and adults, work day after day selling to travelers. The scene in Jipijapa is a drastic departure from the one at the terminal in Guayaquil, where most of the food options include global brands such as McDonald's and KFC. Indeed, following a renovation in 2007, the Guayaquil terminal now looks more like a shopping center than a bus terminal—a clear sign of the growing US commercial influence in Ecuador.

A dusty ride south from Jipijapa takes you to the coast of Manabí. The southern Manabí region is decidedly rural, characterized by rolling hills and dense tropical vegetation in the form of both humid and dry tropical forests. Where the rugged hill region of the coast meets the Pacific Ocean, there are numerous natural bays on which many of the area's towns and villages are located. The bus passes through a number of small port towns as it makes a long curve toward the ocean and a steady decline as it reaches Salango. The two-lane highway parallels the ocean and passes the local cemetery just before the bus comes to a jarring stop at the edge of town. Local residents quickly jump off the bus while others wait to climb on. It is a rarity to see anyone other than locals get on or off the bus in Salango, unless they are part of a student group that conducts field projects in the area or the occasional missionary who visits local households, something that is occurring with increasing frequency. The community is situated on a protected bay where low-lying hills meet the Pacific Ocean, and it is bisected by the coastal highway. A single paved road leads from the highway to the beach, and bicycles are far more common than automobiles. On any given afternoon one can witness children playing soccer in the streets while women converse on the stoops of their brightly colored homes and men congregate at the beachfront. In many ways Salango is a typical Ecuadorian fishing village, and *tranquilo* (tranquil) is the word most locals use to describe the community. However, significant changes have occurred since the early 2000s. This book is about these changes and the lives of the residents of the rural fishing community that is situated along Ecuador's Pacific Coast.

THEORETICAL CONCERNS

Two prominent themes emerged throughout my time spent in Salango: identity and development. I approach both with reference to how locals understand the past and the archaeological record while also emphasizing how a seemingly remote community is integrated into national and international discussions about identity and development. Moreover, my experiences suggest that what I witnessed in Salango stands in contrast to dominant homogenizing discourses on identity that have been historically prominent throughout Latin America.

I approach identity through the framework presented by Hill and Wilson that emphasizes the distinction between "identity politics" and the "politics of identities" (Hill and Wilson 2003). The former represents dominant, often top-down or state-mediated processes by which particular identities are given preference over, and deemed more appropriate than, subaltern identities. The latter refers to bottom-up processes, whereby traditionally marginalized or silenced identities are promoted as a means of challenging the hegemonic structures that favor a particular identity or set of identities.

Mestizaje is the most prevalent paradigm of identity politics in Latin America. It is an ideology that promotes cultural and racial mixing toward an ultimate goal of achieving a set of cultural, and in some cases phenotypical, characteristics associated with "whiteness" or European-ness. The ideology of mestizaje has origins in the colonial conquest of the Americas and the mixing of Indigenous, African, and Spanish peoples, both biologically and culturally. A vast literature exists with reference to mestizaje, and seminal contributions include that of Mexican author and educator José Vasconcelos. In his book *La Raza Cósmica*, Vasconcelos (1925) promotes mestizaje as a founding ideology of Latin American identity: "The lower types of the species will be absorbed by the superior type . . . the uglier stocks will give way to the more beautiful. Inferior races, upon being educated, would become less prolific, and the better specimens would go on ascending a scale of ethnic improvement" (30–31).[2] The result of this mixing, per Vasconcelos, is mestizo identity, an identity "made of the treasury of all of the previous races, the final race, the cosmic race" (41). As alluded to in the work of Vasconcelos, mestizo identity, which is the product of mestizaje, occurs through acquiring markers *associated* with progress and modernity, including education, literacy, urban-ness, and mastery of the Spanish language. At the same time, *perceived* markers of indigeneity, such as traditional clothing, language, rural-ness, illiteracy, and lack of formal education, are viewed as having little value in contributing to a mestizo identity and society at large. Multiple scholars refer to the associated process as *blanqueamiento* (whitening) (Whitten 2003b; Whitten and Fine 1981; Whitten and Quiroga 1998). Thus, mestizo identity is a mixed identity that privileges a certain cultural form over all others and that is reinforced in the everyday interactions of many Latin Americans.

A fundamental component of the paradigm of mestizaje is the ability for individuals to achieve a mestizo identity through adopting the appropriate cultural markers and abandoning markers that are of lesser value. For example, Clara is a young woman in her early twenties of Indigenous Kichwa descent who now resides in Guayaquil. She and her mother own a small mini-market in an upscale residential neighborhood on the outskirts of the city. I became acquainted with Clara a number of years ago when I would visit family in Guayaquil and go to the mini-market for produce or other daily needs. At the time, Clara wore traditional Kichwa clothing, including a long skirt and an embroidered white blouse. She would speak with her mother in Kichwa and rarely looked customers in the eye. By all accounts, Clara was Indigenous, and a marked social distance existed between her and the middle- to upper-middle-class mestizos who frequented her family's store. More recently, Clara has taken to wearing blue jeans and T-shirts, and her teeth are being straightened with braces. "Did you notice Clara? She has a mestizo boyfriend, and she is converting herself to mestiza," was part of the commentary shared over lunch after visiting the mini-market earlier in the day. Such statements point to the plasticity of identity in Latin America and to the overwhelming presence of mestizaje in the day-to-day interactions of Ecuadorians.

On a different occasion, in 2009, a few years before I met Clara, I was invited to the home of an acquaintance in one of the most well-to-do residential areas of Guayaquil. The event was New Year's Day, and brunch was served in an elegant dining area that overlooked a vast living room with expansive marble floors and ornate furnishings. As we engaged in conversation, I was asked about my work on the coast and if I knew of a young man from one of the villages who was engaged to marry a young woman from England. "I do, he is from La Palma," I responded as I recalled a previous conversation with Manuel about the upcoming wedding. "They are improving the race on the coast," stated my host in a matter-of-fact manner. Statements such as these are neither new nor rare in Ecuador. Indeed, prominent anthropologist Norman E. Whitten Jr. provides a similar example from a 1972 political speech by past Ecuadorian president Guillermo Rodríguez Lara. The speech was given in the Amazon city of Puyo at a time when Ecuador's Amazonian interior was gaining attention because of a growing petroleum industry: "There is no more Indian problem . . . we all become white when we accept the goals of national culture" (Whitten 1977:183).[3] The examples from my own experiences reflect the everyday manifestations of mestizaje as both ideology and practice, while Whitten's illustration is representative of what we might conceive of as state-sponsored mestizaje in Ecuador. However, in all of the aforementioned cases, mestizaje takes the form of identity politics; it is top-down and imposed upon those in marginalized or subordinate positions. Because of the politics of mestizaje, it is common for individuals to reject the label "Indigenous" in favor of a mestizo identity because the former inhibits socioeconomic mobility while the latter affords such mobility (Martínez Novo 2006).

The politics of identities contrasts with identity politics and is often expressed in the form of counter-hegemonic discourses that aim to valorize peoples and identities that have a history of being marginalized and subjugated. Referencing Rodríguez Lara, Indigenous identities would be one such example of a marginalized or subjugated identity. In fact, in practice, Indigenous Ecuadorians have historically been denied equal access to citizenship rights through forms of structural violence, including the *hacienda* and *huasipungo* systems.[4] However, beginning in the 1940s and with growing awareness in the 1990s, Indigenous Ecuadorians pushed for recognition of Indigenous rights through the formation of a variety of organizations at the local, regional, and national levels. The most prominent is Ecuador's national Indigenous organization, the Confederation of Indigenous Nationalities of Ecuador (CONAIE). CONAIE creates a space and a mechanism for Indigenous political organizing. While the focus of my work is not CONAIE or Indigenous politics at the national level, it is worth mentioning that CONAIE is representative of the politics of identities and has fostered political change in Ecuador. Moreover, CONAIE has challenged a singular view of Ecuadorian history that emphasizes mestizaje and a homogenized image of indigeneity while promoting a history that recognizes the different Indigenous communities that occupy Ecuador (Benavides 2011). This recognition manifests itself in the acknowledgment and promotion of plurinationalism, a theme addressed in depth in chapter 4. As I suggest in the following chapters, the politics of identities is not relegated to formal political institutions or organizational frameworks but instead is expressed through a variety of channels, including ritual practices, communal politics, and symbolic connections to the past.

Ethnicity and ethnogenesis relate to identity politics and the politics of identities in a number of ways. The former refers in part to how people frame their identity in times of conflict (A. Cohen 1969). The implicit suggestion is that ethnic groups or claims to an ethnic identity represent collective responses to struggle and are instrumental in achieving a particular goal. However, manifestations of ethnicity can take different forms. In some cases, ethnicity is expressed through everyday practices such as language and dress, while in other instances ethnic identity only appears in times of tension and conflict (Sandstrom 2008). For outsiders as well as those who stake claim to a particular ethnic identity, there is often an asserted claim to continuity and the past. Such a primordial approach to ethnic identity suggests that ethnicity is permanent and fundamental to human identity (Banks 1996). While the aforementioned are appropriate for understanding ethnicity, anthropologists have moved beyond a perspective that emphasizes ethnic identity as a cohesive set of cultural traits—including language, ritual, ties to territory, and similar factors—and instead recognize the subjectivity of ethnicity while addressing "specific historical, political, and social contexts of power" as shaping ethnicity (Stephen 1996:32). The issue then becomes not what is "contained" within an ethnic group in terms of defining characteristics but instead how the ethnic group is shaped by outside influences as well as group responses to such influences. If we take this approach, we are left with a focus on the political dimensions of ethnicity while simultaneously recognizing its dynamic and fluid nature. The result of this perspective is the acknowledgment that ethnic identity can be used for instrumental purposes and is often the result of strategic constructions that allow people to be successful and to prosper (Sandstrom 2008).

Ethnogenesis is the creation or assertion of a collective identity (Sandstrom 2008), and it relates to ethnic identity as groups undergoing processes of assimilation and ethnocide partake in adaptive processes to counteract such changes while simultaneously reconfiguring their own symbolic relationships (Whitten 1976). A priority in recent studies of ethnogenesis is to push for recognition of the intersection of local and global processes while at the same time arguing against representations of Native peoples as static and isolated and instead acknowledging the dynamic nature of ethnic identity (see Hill 1996). Ethnogenesis often occurs as two groups come together to create a new ethnic group/identity. In other instances, ethnogenesis occurs when people express an identity that serves to differentiate them from homogenized identities that are the product of historical contact and assimilation. This corresponds closely to Stark and Chance's (2008) position that acknowledges ethnicity as based on a presumed common heritage or a presumed connection to the past. This newly articulated identity often extends beyond any known affinity or relationship and is instead based upon a shared understanding of the past and an asserted connection to the past, however thin the conjoining threads might be.

The recognition that connections to the past might be tenuous brings to bear the question of authenticity as it relates to claims to ethnicity. Relevant contributions to this discussion include the writings of Conklin (1997), French (2004), García and Lucero (2011), Gaytán (2008), Lucero (2006), Morales, Cano, and Mysyk (2004), and Smith (2015). While each provides a valuable contribution to the ongoing debates surrounding ethnic identities, it is not my intention going forward to endeavor to explore questions of authenticity. Instead, I find it useful to follow the perspective of Handler (1986), which recognizes the concept of authenticity as a cultural construct that is largely the product of a Western worldview. Given this, I find it problematic to apply the concept of authenticity to questions of ethnicity, Indigenous or otherwise. The end goal is therefore not to validate or question the relative authenticity of claims to an ethnic identity but instead to provide insight into the ways groups conceive of and negotiate their own identities.

The second dominant theme of this book is development. One of the things that sparked my interest in development in Ecuador was a billboard I passed in Guayas province in 2004. The billboard depicted a stylized image of a rising sun situated behind rolling mountains, with the ocean in the foreground. The rays of the sun were also cast into the foreground, projecting a sense of illuminated hope and prosperity. The words to the left reinforced the imagery: "A single path, a single road . . . the development of the country!" Despite the emphasis on a single development path, development practices vary widely. In general, scholars acknowledge two kinds of development: mainstream and alternative. My goal here is not to provide an exhaustive presentation of development practices or the scholarly literature that analyzes or critiques them. However, it is appropriate to address some of the basic meanings and attributes relevant to the case studies discussed in later chapters.

Like mestizaje, economic development exists as both practice and ideology, and the concept of development has multiple interpretations. On the one hand, economic development can be correlated with economic growth, an increase in exports and foreign trade, and a rise in gross domestic product (GDP). Alternatively, economic development is often understood in terms of improved livelihoods and a reduction in poverty. However, these directives are often obscured as a consequence or perhaps the intent of large bureaucratic institutions, and most critics of mainstream development argue that development serves as a mechanism of economic and social domination through the control of economic resources (see Bebbington 1992 and Escobar 1995, for example). As linked to colonialism and post-colonialism, development, "although couched in terms of humanitarian goals and in the preservation of freedom[,] . . . sought to provide a new hold on countries and their resources" (Escobar 1995:26) by expanding markets and promoting capitalist agendas that replicate colonial relations by driving "developing" nations into cycles of debt and dependence.

Numerous critics place multinational development institutions, including the World Bank and the International Monetary Fund (IMF), at the center of this critique; a brief examination of the Ecuadorian case will illustrate why. The World Bank and the IMF are major multilateral financial institutions that provide loans to developing nations the world over. From a neo-liberal perspective, development is associated with economic growth or progress by way of structural adjustment (Barkin 2001; Bretón Solo de Zaldívar 2002; Escobar 1995). In the 1980s and 1990s, the World Bank and the IMF promoted neo-liberal policies aimed at increasing international trade, financing industry, and making significant investments in developing nations while at the same time pushing for the privatization of public enterprises and limited government interventions and regulations in the name of progress, democracy, and freedom (Sunkel 2005). The latter were means of structural adjustment employed throughout much of Latin America. Critics of such policies point to greater disparities in wealth and increases in poverty as results of neo-liberal reforms (Barkin 2001; Escobar 1995). Simply put, the wealthy grew wealthier and the poor became poorer while developing countries increased their dependency on powerful foreign partners.

In Ecuador, neo-liberal policies preceded a significant economic decline that reached its lowest point in the late 1990s. President Jamil Mahuad Witt embraced neo-liberalism as the country took on significant external debt while decreasing financial regulations and allowing "state and private banks free reign [*sic*] to wheel and deal with millions of dollars of entrusted capital" (Whitten 2003a:2). By 1999 Ecuador had become one of the poorest countries in the Western Hemisphere as the national currency, the sucre, declined in value from 370 sucres per US dollar in 1988 to over 24,000 sucres per US dollar in early 2000 (*Treasury Reporting Rates of Exchange as of March 31, 1988; Treasury Reporting Rates of Exchange as of March 31, 2000*). Wealthy elites who had the capacity to work and invest in US dollars rapidly increased their wealth, while average Ecuadorians became poorer each day as their currency declined in value. Between March and September 2000, the government made a dramatic move and adopted the US dollar as the official currency (Solimano 2002). With an accumulation of debt from multilateral lending institutions, in 2008 Ecuador defaulted on $3.9 billion in foreign debt (Faiola 2008).

Alternative models of development are qualitatively different than mainstream models. Alternative approaches take many forms, often referred to as grassroots and in some cases local economic development (LED). A key component of such models is an emphasis on humanitarian concerns and improved livelihoods. This differs markedly from neo-liberal practices that emphasize economic growth but often overlook local concerns. Binns and Nel, for example, suggest that local economic development appears "to be among the few realistic development options available to the 'poorest of the poor,' who seem to have been all but abandoned by the Western-dominated global economy" (Binns and Nel 1999:390). Bebbington (1997) suggests that alternative practices often take into account culturally appropriate forms of development. A recent perspective, which is a prominent component of this book, is community development.

Examples of alternative models of development include the formation of small-scale economic cooperatives, micro-credits for small-scale entrepreneurs, and similar types of projects. It is often the case that local community members or organizations initiate projects and seek funding from non-governmental organizations (NGOs). In recent years many development organizations that once embodied neo-liberal principles experienced philosophical changes, so development is no longer defined strictly as economic growth. Instead, a more nuanced perspective recognizes local concerns, including a recognition of rights, Indigenous and otherwise, that often challenge a neo-liberal framework (Gordon and Hale 2003). Thus, disentangling mainstream development and alternative development ideologies and practices is more difficult than it once was. However, the main distinction is still largely one of size as well as project implementation. In chapter 5 I provide more detail on this issue through multiple case studies that draw from my experiences with mainstream and alternative development practices, including World Bank–funded development projects in Salango.

Moving forward, I address both mainstream and alternative models for development within the context of Salango. I am most concerned with how development is negotiated at the local level: by the people of Salango. At the same time, I pay close attention to how identity and development are interwoven, particularly as related to questions of mestizaje. A final component that underlies questions of both identity and mestizaje is the presence of the past in the form of the archaeological record and the knowledge residents have about the prehistory of their community. I suggest that identity and development are significantly influenced by local understandings of the past, as perceived connections to the region's prehistory are leveraged in the negotiation of development. Thus, this book is less about economic change and more about the social and cultural transformations associated with development as they relate to localized conceptions of identity.

A final note is that this book was written with students in mind. I gained a deep interest in Latin America in part because of exposure to engaging ethnographies when I was an undergraduate student. I was captivated and inspired by the experiences of ethnographers who wrote about life in rural communities and how people responded to and negotiated the transformations brought forth by living in an increasingly globalized context. It is my hope that this work can provide similar inspiration for students to take an interest in Latin America.

ORGANIZATION OF THE BOOK

Chapter 2 focuses on life in Salango by addressing the local economy, political organization, and social differentiation within the community. I emphasize the local fishing economy as a defining feature of life in Salango. I trace the rise of Salango's fishing economy from a small-scale subsistence-based fishery to the growth of a commercial fishing fleet. I introduce the connections between contemporary practice and localized conceptions of identity while paying special attention to local narratives about changes that have taken place since the 1970s. Throughout this chapter I suggest that local identity is embedded in the cultural practices of work associated with the local fishery. I emphasize that economic practices are not compartmentalized from other domains of culture but instead form the framework for understanding and asserting village identity.

In chapter 3 I address Salango's prehistory and suggest that the prehistory is of fundamental importance for understanding development and identity in Salango. The chapter emphasizes archaeology and community patrimony as important contributors to local identity. Throughout the chapter I focus on the prehistory of the region, as illuminated through the archaeological record, and on contemporary constructions of a place-based identity that leverages the archaeological record. I focus on local conceptions of the pre-Columbian past and on the role material connections, in the form of the archaeological record, play in the everyday lives of Salango residents. In addition, I present two ethnographic examples that illustrate the significance of archaeology with reference to identity in Salango. The first example references the annual festival that celebrates Indigenous heritage and the pre-Columbian *Manteño* population that inhabited the Ecuadorian coast at the time of Spanish contact.[5] The second example comes from the twentieth anniversary celebration of the local archaeology museum.

Chapter 4 highlights the claims to indigeneity in Salango and the associated tensions and subsequent struggles that led to Salango gaining government recognition as an ancestral community in 2004. The underlying theoretical concerns are ethnogenesis and the politics of identity. As such, I situate the case of Salango within the existent literature pertaining to these areas of scholarly interest. In addition, I focus on the concept of the road as both a symbol of and a realistic contributor to the emergence of an ethnic-based discourse in Salango. I suggest that the construction of Ecuador's main coastal highway in the 1970s and the integration of Salango into the regional and national economies served as a conduit for an increased archaeological presence in the region that ultimately played a role in claims of Indigenous identity. I also examine the protests of 2004, when this same highway was blocked to assert claims to territory and government recognition of Indigenous identity. An additional component of the chapter is to contextualize Salangueño claims to an Indigenous identity within the broader cultural context of national politics and constitutional reforms that recognize Ecuador as a plurinational state. In this chapter I bring together ideas about identity, belonging, the politics of identity, and identity politics. I trace recent Indigenous mobilizations in Ecuador, beginning with the *levantamiento indígena* (Indigenous uprising) of 1990, and the expansion of Indigenous politics from the highland and Amazonian regions to the Ecuadorian coast. I also present data on local conceptions of identity. I suggest that there is a difference between identity and belonging; the former has deep political implications, and the latter is about place and a sense of personhood with reference to community. Moreover, I address how identity is a contested terrain linked closely to community politics.

Chapter 5 examines issues of culture change and development in Salango, with special attention paid to how development is negotiated at the local level. I begin by situating Salango within the broader regional context, as related to tourism development. One component of that context is the fact that Salango is located on the outskirts of Ecuador's only coastal national park. As the chapter moves forward, I trace the origins of tourism development in Salango by addressing three cases: the formation of an NGO-sponsored tourism cooperative, a later World Bank–funded communal tourism initiative, and private tourism enterprises in the community. I highlight the difficulties encountered by each of the three approaches while emphasizing the role of the national park in providing both opportunities and challenges.

The final chapter revisits the dominant theme of culture change while simultaneously suggesting that change in Salango follows two lines that are interwoven. The first is change in the form of increased regional and global connectivity by way of increased access to regional and national markets, the growth of the local fishing economy, and an increased outsider presence— including development specialists, tourists, and archaeologists. The second major change is related to ethnic politics at the local and national levels. I conclude that the growth of an ethnic-based discourse among the residents of Salango must be understood not as a uniquely local response to internal political tensions but as informed by the broader context of constitutional reform (chapter 4), regional development (chapter 5), identity politics and the politics of identity (chapter 4), and the perceived continuity between past and present (chapter 3).

NOTES

1. In Ecuador the term *gringo* is not generally used in a derogatory manner, and it is not restricted as a descriptor of North Americans. The term is used to refer to North Americans, Europeans, Australians, and similar groups. The key components of its meaning are light-skinned and foreign.

2. Los tipos bajos de la especie serán absorbidos por el tipo superior. De esta suerte podría redimirse, por ejemplo, el negro, y poco a poco, por extinción voluntaria, los extirpes más feas irán cediendo el paso a las más hermosas. Las razas inferiores, al educarse, se harían menos prolíficas, y los mejores especímenes irán ascendiendo en una escala de mejoramiento étnico (Vasconcelos 1925:30–31). All translations are by the author.

3. No hay más problema en relación con los indígenas . . . todos nosotros pasamos a ser blancos cuando aceptamos las metas de la cultura nacional (Whitten 1977:183).

4. The term *hacienda* refers to a landed estate. As a system, the hacienda allowed for control of land and resources, including the labor resources of Indigenous peoples residing on hacienda lands. The term *huasipungo* refers to a relationship of tenancy and debt peonage associated with Indians living on hacienda lands.

5. I provide a similar account in an article published in the *Revista de Antropología Experimental* (Bauer 2010b), and Smith addresses the same issue in her more recent book on the coastal Ecuadorian community of Agua Blanca (Smith 2015).

2

Community, Economy, and Identity

Salango is a community of contrasts. The topography of the region provides for a natural bay that serves as the western boundary of the village. Low-lying hills rise sharply from the Pacific Ocean, resulting in a distinct micro-climate in which temperatures vary significantly throughout the year as dense cloud cover and light rain give way to the intense rays of the equatorial sun. The local climate is generally characterized by a cool, damp season from June through September and a hotter and dryer season from November through May. The area, characterized as a "moisture-trap zone" by Harris and colleagues (2004), experiences a persistent light rain known locally as *garua* during the months of June through September. The annual cycle of rainy weather is a welcome sight for villagers, and it is not uncommon for the garua to hang over the village for consecutive days while often turning into a harder rain at night. The dusty streets change to mud, and the forested hills become abundantly green. Temperatures increase dramatically from November through May, and residents respond to the sweltering heat by seeking refuge inside their homes or in any of the shaded hammocks strung throughout the village.

I learned early in my fieldwork that the contrasts present in Salango extend beyond those readily visible in the natural environment and include complementary political institutions and social differentiations based on wealth and class. These contrasts increasingly drew

DOI: 10.5876/9781607327608.c002

24

FIGURE 2.1. *Salango looking to the north*

my attention and are of relevance for understanding the case study presented in this book.

It was 2003. The rain was unseasonably heavy the day Diego and his cousin Mario invited me to walk with them to a small restaurant located along the *malecón* (boardwalk). "We are going to register," Mario told me with excitement as he moved quickly along the muddy street, a noticeable eagerness in his step. Mario was a young man, close to my age. He and Diego grew up together because their mothers are sisters and Mario's father had been absent since he was a child. Mario had a bit of wild streak about him, even though or perhaps because he became the man of the house at a young age. He had a sly grin, sharp wit, and fiery temper. He grew up hard and worked in the ocean with his uncle and cousins. His teenage years were spent traveling to and from the Galapagos Islands to work as a diver during the months of sea cucumber and lobster harvest, and he often shared the difficulties of the work, which required him to be in the frigid Pacific waters for hours at a time, only to rest at the end of the day in a crowded bunk room on the mother vessel as it moved to a new dive site for work the following day.

When he was in Salango, Mario was generally free from the stresses and worries he had in the islands. However, he would frequently talk about returning and about his goal to move there and establish himself permanently—a goal he would eventually achieve through a series of fortuitous events that allowed him to gain residency on the islands. However, in 2003 Mario was unsettled and always seemed to be looking for something. Perhaps it was anger he harbored toward his deceased father, something he often reflected upon with sadness and animosity when he was drinking; or maybe it was his desire to have the family he had never had. No matter the cause, Mario was searching.

"Register . . . for what?" I asked. "The *comuna*," responded Mario with excitement. "We have to sign; today is the day to register." The comuna is a political body and the minimal legal administrative unit present in Ecuador. It is a community council of sorts. Comunas are associated mostly with rural areas, and they are more common in the Indigenous highland and Amazon regions than on the Ecuadorian coast. The institutional origins of the comuna can be traced to the 1937 *Ley de Organización y Régimen de Comunas* (commonly known as the Ley de Comunas, or Law of Communes). The law established a legal framework for the organization of Indigenous and peasant communities in Ecuador by extending legal recognition to them while at the same time providing a formal organizational structure to allow for government oversight of such populations (Becker 1999). Rural communities could establish a comuna through the organization of fifty or more members and the filing of the appropriate paperwork with the Ecuadorian Ministry of Agriculture. In this original form, the comuna provided little direct benefit to communities but did function to provide legal recognition and allow for government oversight of communities by way of documenting demography (Cervone 2012).

Comunas consist of a *cabildo*, or council, and the general assembly, which is made up of *comuneros*. The term *comuneros* refers to individuals belonging to Indigenous communities with ties to communal lands (*terrenos comunales*) (Becker 1999) or ancestral lands (*terrenos ancestrales*). Despite the current focus on land as a legitimizing component of the comuna, land was not an original consideration in the 1937 law, and it was not until nearly thirty years later that agrarian reform laws passed in 1964 and 1973 sought to deliver land to un-landed peasants through the expropriation of hacienda lands (Colloredo-Mansfeld 2002). Today, the resultant communal lands are administered by comunas, and the responsibility for oversight and protection of communal lands falls to the comuna. The issue of ancestral land will be discussed in more detail in forthcoming chapters.

The comuna Salango was formed in 1976. It includes Salango and the neighboring village of Río Chico. However, despite having access to land, it was not until 1991 that the comuna was granted communal title to 2,536 hectares (6,266 acres) of land that extends from the northernmost point of Salango to the southernmost point of the village of Río Chico and inland to an area known as Platanales.

Despite the gloomy day in which the dull pastel colors of the ocean and sky came together under the muffled daylight, Mario was upbeat, almost giddy. At the time, I did not understand the significance of the moment, but much later it would be marked in my mind as a catalyst for what was to come. We hustled through the rain and reached the cement steps of the small open-air restaurant. A few individuals were present, saying goodbyes as we entered. "Don Adolfo, doña Estela," Mario said with a nod of his head and a show of respect as two elder community members passed by on their way out. "Young man," the woman commented. "Clavo," stated her husband, while nodding his head toward Mario. Clavo is Mario's apodo, and most people throughout the community refer to him that way. Sitting behind a small wooden table was a gentleman wearing a collared shirt, blue jeans, and a black leather jacket. With his dark hair slicked back and his beard trimmed yet rugged, he looked different from most community members. "*Compañeros*, how are you?" he said with an air of confidence as he stood up to firmly shake our hands. "Young men, are you here to sign? Please, please, right here." He slid a paper across the table for Diego and Mario to read and sign. The paper was a petition that would serve as the foundation for an ongoing struggle to denounce the cabildo that was in place and in effect to reestablish the comuna with a new cabildo, including the role of president to be held by the man in the leather jacket.

We did not stay and talk; it was merely sign and leave, but it did seem important. "Who is he?" I asked as we left. Certainly, there was something up, all the excitement and then just a signature. "He is Roberto Toledo," responded Diego. That did not mean anything to me at the time. I would learn throughout my experiences in Salango that questions are often answered with what many Americans might think of as insufficient or maybe even inappropriate responses. For example, when passing someone on the street in Salango, it is common courtesy to address them, even with a simple "how are you?" The response is very often "walking." This does answer the question, but not in a manner that meets the expectations of most Americans.

"Yes, but who is he?" I asked again. "He wants to be the new president of the comuna," Diego replied in short. "Why?" I inquired. "There are lots of problems. The people are not happy . . . the people want a change," he asserted. The dissatisfaction with the local political situation and the desire for change would continue to manifest themselves throughout my research, and the themes would become far more significant than I imagined during that brief explanation provided by Diego. In later conversations I would learn that Toledo was not from Salango but from the city of Guayaquil. He married into a prominent family and moved to the area to seek out a life free from the stresses of an urban existence. For some time, he attempted to live off the land and provide for himself and his family by practicing horticulture. As he became more involved in the comuna, his political motivations increased, either because of his own aspirations or at the suggestion of others, and he would eventually become a powerful local politician who aligned himself with progressive politics and who was either viewed as a local revolutionary or accused of corruption and self-serving politics, depending on who was asked.

Complementary to the comuna is the *parroquia* (parish). The parroquia of Salango was established in 1996 and represents an alternative form of political structure in the community. Parroquias are the minimal administrative unit within the territorial administration of Ecuador and have a direct link to the state. The ordering of territorial administration includes, in ascending order, the parroquia, the *cantón* (provincial capital), and the *provincia* (province). The parroquia exists under the administrative jurisdiction of the cantón of Puerto López (pop. 15,000). The parroquia of Salango includes six communities with a combined population of approximately 4,000 individuals.

The parroquia is made up of elected officials, as is the comuna, and its primary function is as a form of local representation for the cantón of Puerto López. Unlike the comuna, the parroquia is not responsible for access to and maintenance of communal land. Instead, the parroquia is charged with linking Salango and associated communities to the regional, provincial, and national governments. Ultimately, the comuna and the parroquia are separate entities entrusted with very different responsibilities. However, they have a tense relationship as they jostle for position to attain local political and social power. Adding to this complexity is the fact that, historically, the parroquia has garnered the support of the most powerful fishing families in the community of Salango, whereas the comuna has historically garnered support from comuneros from Río Chico as well as individuals from Salango who have a vested interest in the use of communal lands. Thus, the comuna and the parroquia symbolize the internal differences of class and economic practice that define Salango. These distinctions would prove relevant throughout my time in the field, with the comuna dominating the local political landscape and also being a central feature of local development efforts and claims about identity.

DEMOGRAPHY AND STATUS: THE
CONSTITUTION OF COMMUNITY

To the outside observer, Salango appears to be a village where life moves at a relaxed pace and changes are slow to come. Hammocks made of fish nets hang from trees surrounding the cement soccer field at the north end of town, and residents spend afternoons relaxing by playing cards, talking with friends, and participating in sports, including *fútbol* (soccer) and *voli* (a modified version of volleyball). A preliminary map and census I conducted in 2002 accounts for approximately 300 households and roughly 1,400 fulltime residents in the village. A census conducted by the parroquia indicates that there were 2,082 residents in the community of Salango in the same year. These numbers were still relatively consistent at the time of this writing. However, population estimates for Salango vary, largely because of population movement, and an accurate population estimate is very difficult to establish because there is a fairly consistent flow of individuals in and out of the community.

Migration is extremely common in Ecuadorian society. While specific numbers of Ecuadorians living abroad are difficult to estimate, Weismantel (2003:331) characterizes the condition of Ecuadorian migration as one in which "Ecuadorians from all walks of life abandon the land of their birth for the United States." Pribilsky (2007:9) uses the phrase "massive exodus" to refer to the movement of Ecuadorians from the highland Azuayo-Cañari region to the United States while estimating that nearly 600,000 Ecuadorians lived in the United States at the time of the 2000 US Census.[1] It is so common for Ecuadorians to live abroad that, at the time of my earliest research, the national newspaper *El Universo* regularly published letters from Ecuadorians living outside the country. Many locals shared stories with me about friends and family who lived abroad, and numerous residents of Salango shared stories about their own time living abroad for extended periods. Most people with whom I spoke about migration cited economic opportunity or a lack thereof as the primary motivator for leaving Ecuador. This was especially true during the period of catastrophic economic decline that characterized the 1990s.[2] The devaluation of Ecuador's currency, the sucre, created a high level of economic uncertainty, resulting in many residents leaving the country in search of increased economic opportunities. At the time of this writing, residents of Salango are living and working in Venezuela, Spain, Germany, the United States, and the island nation of Curaçao. There is also a strong presence of Salangueños in the Ecuadorian cities of Jipijapa, Portoviejo, Guayaquil, Quito, Manta, and the Galapagos Islands. In most cases these movements are precipitated by a desire to improve economic opportunities through entry into the formal economy, a situation that is becoming increasingly common with younger generations who are moving away from their natal community to seek better access to education, often at the university level, that will improve their positioning in the job market.

People are not just leaving Salango; people are also moving to the community. This is not entirely new. Many families came to the community within the past fifty years or so, as the growth of the local fishing economy provided opportunities for economic gain and stability. Other families with a longer history in the community recall an ancestor from Mexico coming to Salango on a whaling vessel in the late 1800s. McEwan and colleagues (2006) cite early Spanish sources that indicate that a single family inhabited the village in the late sixteenth century. Moreover, nobody in Salango is a native speaker of an Indigenous language. Despite this, there are individuals and families that claim a primordial connection to Salango. Even so, what is clear is that Salango is made up of a diverse group of people, not all of whom have a long-standing connection to the village. These differences relate, at least in part, to status in the community. Individuals and families with high socioeconomic status are those who have experienced success in the local fishing economy. They are successful boat owners who have the financial means to own cars and boats and to maintain connections to Ecuador's coastal urban centers, including Manta and Guayaquil.

I met Julio in 2005 when he first came to Salango to work in the local fishing industry. At a local *cantina*, he approached Diego and asked for a cigarette. Julio informed us that he had come from Santa Elena to the south and was looking for work. There are some fishing communities throughout the Santa Elena peninsula, but most of the small villages along the coast do not have protected bays, therefore limiting the capacity for a successful fishing industry. Where the coastline is straight or the depth of the ocean decreases dramatically off the shoreline, violent waves and dangerous currents make the prospects of coming and going from shore extremely dangerous. In contrast, Salango enjoys a protected bay in which the depth of the ocean gradually increases as one moves away from the shore. This allows for greater predictability of ocean currents, and the waves in Salango tend to be small, except for an occasional period of *aguaje* (uncharacteristically strong waves).

Julio was twenty years old when he came to Salango. Since that time, his entire family has relocated, including his father, mother, brother, and sister. Julio and his brother began working on a fishing boat and eventually saved up enough money to buy their own small boat and motor. Julio married and welcomed his first child a few years after first arriving in Salango, and he worked hard to build a small home of bamboo and wood with a thatched roof. Salango's fishing economy drew Julio and his family to the village, and he was able to start to make a living for himself and his young family.

Prestige and wealth define status in Salango. While to the outsider the community might appear to be a homogeneous society of rural peasants and fishers, considerations such as family reputation, occupation, and education all play a role in social rank within the community. Although most village residents do not explicitly recognize differences in social class or status, differences do exist, and they play out in everyday interactions between individuals. The most apparent division that exists is based on wealth and reputation associated with economic success in the local fishing industry. Successful fishing families are set apart from other members of the community, and their status is reflected in social interactions and material and labor conditions.

Don Francisco—a member of a prominent fishing family—invited Diego, Manuel, Gustavo, and me to attend the Festival of San Pedro and San Pablo with him in the nearby fishing town of Machalilla. The festival, which is rooted in Catholic religious tradition, celebrates the patron saints with a parade and a blessing of local fishing boats. Don Francisco did not invite us to attend the daily activities, which include the blessing of boats and a regatta, but instead to attend the nighttime *fiesta* that celebrates the saints with music, drinking, and dancing and which differs markedly from the official Catholic version of the celebration.

Catholicism is prominent in Salango, and the community is home to a Catholic Church as well as an Evangelical Church. While my research did not focus on religion, I became familiar with the role of religion in the life of the community and its residents. Even though the majority of Salangueños are Catholic, religious activity is most strongly associated with formal rituals such as baptism, marriage, and death, as well as the numerous festivals that celebrate patron saints. Weekly mass is rarely attended by more than a dozen or so individuals, most of whom are elderly. In contrast to Catholicism, there are a growing number of practitioners of Evangelism and an increasing number of Jehovah's Witnesses. In both cases religion is marked less by important rituals and festivities and more by daily practices such as Bible study. I learned this on multiple occasions when I was invited to lunch or dinner at the home of my *compadre* (co-father) Pedro, only for us to be visited by Jehovah's Witnesses shortly after we finished our meal. The missionaries were sometimes from the United States, other times from Australia—all gringos in the eyes of locals. On each occasion they tried to convince me to stay and partake in Bible study. I declined each request after engaging in a few moments of conversation with my new acquaintances. There was something uncomfortable about the situation and what were seemingly scheduled "drop-in" visits planned in part around my being there. Despite my discomfort with the situation, I noted the ease with which the missionaries were welcomed into the homes of local residents. This was likely because they were gringos much like myself and were therefore viewed with curiosity and interest by some locals.

Despite the religious diversity that is present in Salango, I was never witness to any religious tension in the community. People of different faiths participated together in the numerous important social institutions, including the comuna, the parroquia, school organizations, and economic activities. This is not to suggest that people interacted with absolute harmony; it is merely an assertion that religious differences had no clear correlation to other measures of diversity within the community and did not appear to play an identifiable role in tensions there.

Our attendance at the festival with don Francisco was important for los hermanos because don Francisco is *un duro* (a person of great importance) in Salango. Don Francisco is a member of Salango's most respected fishing family. At the time he was also a prominent regional elected official. Don Francisco was one of the first residents of Salango to own a vehicle other than a *camioneta* (pickup truck). His possession of an SUV was a status symbol, as camionetas are work vehicles that are loaded with fish, gravel, sacks of cement, lumber, and other materials, whereas an auto or an SUV represents a luxury item that does not have the raw, practical functionality associated with camionetas. Moreover, don Francisco traveled frequently to Guayaquil for business and leisure, he drank fine Scotch whiskey, and he had a reputation for frolicking with young women half his age. He placed high-dollar bets on neighborhood voli matches and refused to play with or against anyone other than those he deemed to be the strongest players. He always dressed in a pressed and collared shirt and slacks, except when he was playing voli. Don Francisco was someone to be seen with and to admire. He represented the privileged side of Salango. With all this in mind, we could not turn down the invitation.

We left Salango after 8:00 p.m. Don Francisco and two of his brothers rode in the front of one of the family's camionetas while los hermanos and I, along with a few other invitees, rode in the bed. The choice of the camioneta was purely functional. It would allow for the most passengers, even if the ride was a bit harrowing as we sped through the dark of night along the winding coastal highway. At the fiesta we met some of don Francisco's colleagues and took our seats up front near the music. Despite the fact that don Francisco was a person of prominence, we sat on the same uncomfortably small wooden stools as everyone else, and we huddled around a small unbalanced wooden table that was no different from the tables used by all others in attendance.

Like most public festivals in rural Ecuador, the fiesta was attended by the majority of the community as well as residents from other communities, like ourselves. *Cumbia* music played loudly over the thumping speakers as couples danced under the dim moonlight. Don Francisco ordered round after round of beers and each time pulled a large wad of cash out of his pocket to pay. The smallest thing such as drinking beer at a community festival was an opportunity to note differences in social status. Whereas most residents of Salango order a single bottle of *Pilsener*—the national brand that comes in large 750 milliliter bottles—and drink from a single bottle poured into individual glasses, don Francisco ordered individual cans for each person in his party.

Throughout the night, the conversation was limited because of the noise from the music. The pulsing sound of the heavy beats drowned out the nearby surf as it crashed onto the shore. When conversation did occur, it was most frequently led by don Francisco and consisted of comments about the beauty of young women in attendance and his sexual prowess. Included in this was his advice to seek out a young woman with "*cero kilómetros, cómo un carro nuevo*" (0 kilometers, like a new car). Don Francisco is representative of one segment of Salango, and *machismo* is an important marker of status. How he positioned himself with reference to los hermanos and the other invitees is relevant. He reinforced his status by ordering individual beers for each of us, exposing a wad of cash each time he paid, and talking about women and cars and referencing both of them as material possessions to be had by the dominant male.

Los hermanos always maintained a level of respect for, if not looked up to, don Francisco because of the possibility of improving their own status by interacting with him. Perhaps accepting his invitation would result in future employment opportunities or political favors. Regardless of the outcome of the interactions, los hermanos recognized that their collective status was lower than that of don Francisco and his family, but the potential for upward mobility existed.

Don Marcos represents a similar case of social status in Salango. Don Marcos is also from a successful and extensive fishing family. Unlike don Francisco, he has not been involved in local politics, and his presence in his family's fishing enterprise is more readily visible. Whereas don Francisco is rarely seen mending nets or taking part in the laborious tasks associated with fishing, don Marcos frequently spends time sitting on the beach with a net spread over his lap, mending holes and tears. He works alongside hired

FIGURE 2.2. *Mending nets*

day laborers who spread nets wide between their legs with their toes poked through the mesh and expertly sew the holes with a quick pass of thick nylon thread. Don Marcos is less conspicuous at social gatherings and community festivities, but he tends to be dressed as well as don Francisco. He is noticeably more reserved but still represents one of the most prominent and well-to-do families in Salango.

On one occasion, los hermanos and I found ourselves stranded in Puerto López without gasoline to return to Salango. It was about 10:00 p.m., and we went to Puerto López to see the holiday festivities leading up to Christmas. We had gone in Gustavo's camioneta, but, as is common in Salango, he had only put a gallon of gasoline in the vehicle earlier in the day. Salango does not have a *gasolinera* (gas station), and the one in Puerto López frequently experienced shortages. As such, most people, Gustavo included, would purchase gasoline from a local resident who had managed to procure a small amount, 50 gallons or so, for resale. However, at this moment we were without gasoline, and there was no means of getting any. The malecón was full of people and vehicles. Most of the festivities had come to a close, but people congregated, conversing and walking along the beachfront. We walked around for a few minutes, wading through the mass of people, and saw don Marcos parked just down the street. He was standing next to his camioneta. "We should ask don Marcos" I said to Manuel. He shook his head and said no, then lifted his head to look further into the crowd. I pled my case by asking him why not and telling him that don Marcos would certainly let us siphon a small amount from his tank. After all, he was from Salango, and everybody in Salango knows everybody else. Manuel relented after a little more pressure. We approached don Marcos, and he greeted us with disinterest. To the best of my knowledge, Manuel and don Marcos did not have any personal problems. Their families were not feuding. In fact, don Marcos's son was a close friend of Manuel's, and we had all played together in a soccer match earlier in the week.

Don Marcos turned us away. His rejection was likely an indication of status and his unwillingness to see Manuel and me on equal terms. Manuel had recognized this in advance, and for that reason he was resistant to asking for don Marcos's help.

The types of interactions experienced with don Francisco and don Marcos are not the only indicators of different levels of social status in Salango; individuals of lowest status are often marginalized by other members of the community. Distance plays out in social as well as economic terms. For example, while high-status individuals tend to be boat owners, the lowest-status individuals tend to work not on boats but as laborers transporting fish from the boats to shore by carrying large plastic bins full of fish on their shoulders. They work for minimal pay and often receive a small portion of the catch, in most cases no more than a few small fish, for household consumption.

Maní and his five brothers live in a two-story house of mixed brick and wood located along the beachfront. Although they are all adults, the brothers reside together, and all of them work as *gaveteros* transporting fish from boats to the shore. Maní can often be found hanging out along the malecón alone or with his brothers but rarely with anyone outside his immediate family. When money allows, he spends time at the local store/cantina owned by don Gallo. The store, with its brightly painted facade adorned with political posters and posters of scantily clad women promoting beer and caña (a local liquor made from sugarcane), is a local hangout for drinking, playing cards, and conversing. Maní sits alone, away from the other men at the store, and rarely interacts with them. He usually drinks caña, which is cheaper than beer. He listens to the conversations around him but is hesitant to speak.

As people come and go throughout the evening, it is common practice to offer a small glass of beer to friends and acquaintances and occasionally to people sitting at a nearby table. Maní is rarely included in this ritual of inclusion and recognition. Maní is in many ways an outsider in his own community, and his social position is representative of the diversity of perspectives that exist in Salango.

ECONOMIC PRACTICE AND DAILY LIFE

Social and economic differences in Salango have a strong association with the local fishing economy, and I learned early on that fishing and its associated labor are embedded in the daily practices of life in the village. A look out to the bay or a stroll along the malecón reveals the importance of the local fishing industry. There were thirteen *barcos pesqueros* (fishing boats, also known locally as *chinchorreros*) and numerous *fibras* (fiberglass boats ranging in size from 5 meters to 9 meters) owned by local fishing families at that time my research began in 2002. Since then, the number of barcos has increased, and it is not uncommon to see new boats being built on or near the beach. The fishing industry is the driving force behind the local economy, and the majority of the population of Salango relies almost exclusively on activities related to fishing and diving as primary generators of income. As a consequence, life in the village is inextricably linked to the Pacific Ocean.

The intimate familiarity with the ocean possessed by many Salango residents is cultivated at an early age, when children become intimately aware of the importance of fishing to the community's livelihood. On numerous occasions I was reminded of this by some of the youngest members of the village. I often encountered my young *ahijado* (godson) upon entering his family's home for breakfast early in the morning. As was common practice, I would ask him where his father was. The four-year-old would turn to me with excitement and say, "My daddy is fishing." At the time, Manuel worked closely with his father-in-law. Sometimes he would put out nets, but more often than not he brought fish in from the larger barcos and transported them to shore. It was a common occurrence for Manuel's father-in-law, don Jorge, to come to the house in the early morning to wake Manuel and alert him of the opportunity to work for a few hours. By the time Manuel's son had reached five years of age, he had made his first journeys into the water with his father. For many young boys, work on the family vessel began before age ten.

A great deal has changed in Salango since I first began conducting research in 2002, but the Pacific Ocean remains a consistent presence, not only as a prominent feature of the natural environment but also as a contributing component to the local economy and identity. One of the things that drew me to Salango was the ocean. More specifically, I had a strong interest in the relationship between local residents and the ocean. I was and am still fascinated with how people respond to the natural environment, and admittedly, I am partial to a materialist perspective when addressing questions related to my research. However, I do not subscribe to materialism in any strict or dogmatic sense; instead, my work in Salango is framed by an understanding that activities of

FIGURE 2.3. *Chinchorreros in the bay*

production, viewed in terms of work and relationship to the natural environment, influence identity and worldview while also serving as a foundation for a shared sense of belonging. As such, outlining the basic components of the economy of Salango is central to what is forthcoming in this book.

The economic history of southern Manabí province has undergone numerous transformations since the early twentieth century. Early artisanal fishing along the southern Manabí coast was largely relegated to the use of canoes and small wooden rowboats. The best account of early fishing practices in Salango comes from research conducted by Southon (1985), and much of my own research confirms the information he presents.

Salango's early twentieth-century economy consisted of horticultural production along with fishing. Most elders in the community can vividly recount a time in which horticulture was a salient feature of the local economy. During this period, the village was part of a hacienda known as El Tropical. As was the case throughout much of Ecuador during the early twentieth century, society was highly stratified, and *patrones* maintained a position of authority over the lower-class *peones*. In the late nineteenth century, the hacienda included 620 hectares of pasture, over 60 hectares of sugarcane, and 5,000 coffee bushes. From 1897 to 1907 the number of productive coffee bushes increased from 5,000 to 25,000, and coffee was the dominant cash crop throughout much of Manabí province (Southon 1985). Coffee helped build the cities of Jipijapa and Montecristi, where bustling markets and coffee warehouses filled the downtown sectors. Today, the warehouses are nearly barren, and the cities are a shadow of their former glory. In Salango, coffee production never rose to the same prominence that it did further north in the inland areas. However, many residents remember working in coffee fields as children and young adults, and some still produce coffee in small amounts for household consumption.

Fishing and diving, in contrast, were and still are prominent in Salango. The earliest recorded forms of fishing in the village used the beach seine, and early diving was free diving without compressed air. This form of diving is known locally as *al pulmón* and is still practiced today. The beach seine fishing economy reached its peak during the period between 1930 and 1950, and the nets continued to be used with some frequency until the 1980s (Southon 1985). On occasion, small beach seine were used in the earliest years of my fieldwork.[3] At the same time beach seines were used, offshore fishing took place using small rowboats, known locally as *bongos*. Community elders recount the practice of paddling the bongos into the channel between the mainland and the island. One or more individuals would climb to the top of the island and act as spotters. Once the fish were located, the *red* (net) would be released into the water. The bongo would circle around to entrap the fish, and the full net would then be gathered back into the bongo. Recollections of this type of fishing are presented with a strong sense of nostalgia, of the good old days in Salango, and it is commonplace not only for elders to recall their own experiences of fishing in this way but also for younger generations to pass on the stories told to them by their parents and grandparents while reflecting on the changes that have taken place in their own lifetimes.

Diego shared the following with me as we were anchored off the island on an overcast afternoon in June 2012.

> People always used to fish here at the island. They would put [in] their nets. It was here that they caught lots of *negra*, lots of *albacora*, lots of *bonito*. Fishing was here . . . it was always the fishing and we continue fishing today . . . It used to be very different. Now people use the technology. They use more technology. The [technologies] they use are apparatuses to detect the fish. There is a type called a sonar. That can detect, what do I know? . . . Around about 5 kilometers. And you have the apparatus, "Shoot, there are the fish." And [move] fast to the location. So, the technology is helping. Now with your eyes, you really do not see the fish. The bad thing is, the boats are getting bigger. They run all over the place. They say that fishing is going to fall, any day falling, falling, falling.[4]

I encountered reflections similar to those Diego made with great frequency in Salango. This is in part because most, if not all, of the adult residents had experienced the significant changes associated with the local economy. Don Paulo is one such individual. I established a close friendship with don Paulo and his family over the years, and we would often sit in his home and chat about all things related to fishing and diving. This included stories about his youth and his first experiences with the ocean, the history of the local fishery, and fish stories.

> There used to be a lot of fish; now, only occasionally. It is like all things. There were weeks where we would catch . . . eight to ten *quintales* of *corvina* in a week. When I first began fishing we sold all of the fish to a man in [the village of] Puerto Rico. We would sell, there were *oscuros* where we would sell twenty to thirty quintales. What happened is that we would turn the catch in to him. He would come early in the morning to pay us little by little. We sold lots of fish. Before, when there were lots of corvina, we would fish all night, all night until the morning came [bringing arm from side to side to indicate the length of time spent fishing]. Now, no. Now to catch corvina, two hours would be a lot of time, a lot. Or sometimes in less than an hour a boat passes and it is like there are no fish. They scare the fish. The other day we were there fishing for corvina. There were big ones. We were just arriving and a boat passed [moving arm across his body as though wiping a window clean]. No more.[5]

Don Paulo fishes like many locals who do not have access to the capital needed for a large boat and the associated equipment. The reality is that a select few, like the families of don Francisco and don Marcos, have the economic means to own one of the dozen or so chinchorreros in Salango. The boats now require an investment of US$100,000 or more, and this is not possible for most of the people living in the village. Those who do own boats are local elites or, at a minimum, they represent an economically and socially elevated segment of society. Don Paulo is not a member of this group, and for him and many others in Salango, fishing has changed little from what was done years ago. The fishing entails using a line, hook, and weight. It is fishing by hand over a particular site, or *bajo*, known to have a high concentration of fish.

Unlike most fishermen in Salango, don Paulo also fishes using a rod and reel. I have accompanied him on numerous trips to the rocky outcrops that extend from the mainland toward the island. The rocks are jagged and the surf rushes in, requiring that a person time the tide correctly to have an adequate window for fishing. It is a dangerous endeavor that most locals do not attempt, and my own mettle is tested each time I go. Don Paulo treats me with precaution as I gingerly traverse the rocky outcrops, clinging to them to avoid falling onto the rocks and surf below.

FIGURE 2.4. *Author negotiating the rocks and tide on a fishing trip with don Paulo*

These are the same rocks don Paulo leaps from, scurries up, and negotiates with ease while both of his hands are occupied carrying multiple fishing rods and gear. Truth be told, he usually carries my fishing rod as well to allow me to have both hands free for balance and negotiation of the rocks. Don Paulo fishes with his son and grandson and occasionally his wife and granddaughter. This is a rarity in a village where activities associated with the ocean are dominated almost entirely by men.

The fishing that I learned came from friends of mine from Guayaquil. They first came here asking who catches corvina here. People told them by my apodo, because here people use apodos, Maestro. They said to show them who I was. One day they saw me and said, "Hola, Maestro," and we began talking. They said, "We want to fish for corvina," and we went [motioning as though using a hand line]. In that time there were lots of corvina [big reflective smile]. And we went and we caught about thirty corvina [arms wide showing big size, a big smile on his face]. They were very happy, and I was watching them fishing with a fishing pole [grabs a small wooden plank and picks it up and motions as though he was casting] and I thought, "That should not be too hard." A friend of mine who was with us said, "Give it a try." I used one of the poles and tied a small rock on the end of the line, not a hook, and I casted it [motioning again with the plank], and it fell right there close. I thought, "Okay, I am learning." We came here and we ate, and when we were done they told me, "we are going to leave you with a fishing pole," and they gifted me a fishing pole. I said "Thank you." Every afternoon I would leave here and go to the beach and practice with the pole and small stone, like it was a weight [again motioning] and little by little, further and further. Finally, one day I cast it very hard, and it went really far, really hard, and it went [motioning with his arm as though throwing]. I figured it out. Then when they would return, I was good at catching corvina. They came about a month later, and with four or five poles we were all catching corvina. So, I kept fishing that way and one day the reel broke [grabbing the plank and looking while thinking]. I looked at it and thought "this is not something from another world," and I fixed it. I went fishing again, and from then on I would go fishing with a fishing pole, and I stayed with that. And I stayed there, established with that. Later, more came; lots of people would come to fish with poles. One time we caught a *guato*. It was huge. Caught it with a fishing pole, near the rocks [outstretching his arms].[6]

Regardless of the means of fishing or diving, the cultural importance of ocean-based productive activities remains the same, and fishing/diving and the local economy are components of identity and personhood in Salango. In a manner similar to that discussed by Kistler (2014) in her analysis of market activity in Guatemala, personhood and identity in Salango are informed by economic practice. More specifically, exchange networks are used to solidify relationships and establish a sense of self as well as a sense of belonging.

It is through the social relations and experiences associated with economic exchanges and interactions that personhood, or a sense of identity in relation to others, is developed (Kistler 2014). Exchange networks and economic practices in Salango are closely linked to the base or commons of the Pacific Ocean. My use of the terms *base* and *commons* follows the line of thought put forward by Gudeman (2001:27), where "the commons is a shared interest or value" and serves as the foundation of community. It "is the material thing or knowledge a people have in common, what they share," and it "may have community value—as a symbol of identity" (Gudeman 2001:27–28). Thus, economic interaction with the commons, whether through horticulture production, pastoralism, or fishing and diving, "becomes a performance and mark of identity" (Gudeman 2001:47). Based on his work on Indigenous politics in Andean Ecuador, Colloredo-Mansfeld (2009) provides a complementary position by asserting that relationships to the commons legitimize claims to ethnicity. He specifically references Indigenous ties to land and the practice of horticultural activity as markers of ethnic identity. The perspective presented by Gudeman (2001) and shared by Colloredo-Mansfeld (2009) differs from dominant economic and political models of the commons that view the commons in market terms and reference it as independent of or distinct from community. As I venture to show moving forward, the commons in Salango is a foundational component of the constitution of community and identity.

CHANGE AND CONTINUITY

By the 1960s traditional fishing that used a bongo was mostly replaced with the introduction of outboard motors. Gaibor and colleagues (2002) note a threefold increase in the number of active fishers in Salango from 1963 to 1999. Despite changes in technology and increased access to markets, fishing in Salango follows a distinct pattern that has changed little over the last century. As one young fisherman explained:

> The fishermen work with the moon. During the *claro* period the moon is visible all night. During this time people do not fish at night, but some fish during the day. People do not fish at night because the moon reflects off of the water and they cannot see the schools of fish. When people fish on a barco they use lights to spot the fish. When the light hits schools of fish it is reflected back, and they know that fish are present. During the claro period all of the moonlight reflects off of the water, and it is difficult to see the fish. The lights on the boats are ineffective because the moonlight is also being reflected.

During the oscuro period, a period characterized by limited moonlight, a daily routine of gathering on the beach occurs each afternoon. The movement usually begins at about 4:00 p.m. The fishermen make their way down the dirt roads of the village toward the beach. Each crew has its own meeting spot along the malécon. The locations correspond roughly to those of the chinchorreros moored in the bay. Dressed in sweatpants and sweatshirts and carrying small plastic bags containing dinner for the evening, the men anticipate a cold night at sea. Although the trip might only last a few hours, the job entails high degrees of risk and danger. For these reasons it is common to see wives and children accompany their husbands and fathers to the beach each afternoon.

The dangers encountered on the ocean are many. Mistakes can cause injury or worse: the loss of human life. A friend and neighbor of mine nearly lost his finger in the spring of 2006. He was working on his father-in-law's boat when the tension on a pulley was released, sending a large steel *gancho* (hook) slamming down on his left index finger. The force of the impact, which pinned his hand between the gunnel and the gancho, nearly severed his finger. After an emergency trip to the hospital in La Libertad, a three-hour drive to the south, his finger was saved. This story only touches on the severity of the dangers encountered by the fishermen of Salango. Rogue waves have the potential to severely damage the hulls of chinchorreros, and nets caught up on rocks at the bottom of the ocean have been known to pull entire boats under the water as the diesel engine is forced into full throttle in an attempt to tear the nets from the rocks. As one lifelong fisherman related, "This life is extremely difficult, it is very dangerous; one must have a great deal of respect for the ocean. The ocean gives life and it can take life." A message sent to me by Manuel in January 2015 highlights this point. A young boy, nine years of age, was fishing with his family in their fibra. As described by Manuel, it had been an extended period of aguaje, and upon their return in the evening, the fibra was hit by a powerful wave that caused it to capsize. The boy, who often played in the street with other neighborhood children, including Manuel's young children, was thrown overboard and drowned. As I read the message, my heart sank. The tragedy of living life in what many would consider a tropical paradise set against the backdrop of the Pacific Ocean is that work is hard and life is often cut short. For this reason, the ocean is both revered and respected, and stories of good and bad in Salango often emanate from experiences with the ocean.

One of the most prominent stories told in Salango is the story of the *fantasma* (phantom) that inhabits the local island. It is a story I was told in various forms by numerous community members, including Diego, on one of our many trips to the island.

I will tell you. I have heard of the phantom since I was a child. Okay, so many years ago, possibly 150 or more, from the old times, in Salango there were only maybe ten houses. There were only three or four families. Among those was my family from my mother's side, my grandparents, and the father of my grand-father. They told the story that one day a foreigner arrived. Foreigners here are always called gringos because they are white and have lots of [body and facial] hair. People from here have Indigenous blood and racial features, we do not have lots of hair. We are, there are mixtures, but we are not very hairy. And in stature we are not very tall. And in that time the people were even shorter and the foreigners more developed, taller. White skin, hair, different eyes. Therefore, always called gringo. The gringo always carried with him something large, a large box. People say he carried this wooden box. And people thought, "It could be gold or a dead person." People imagined things. He had money, and here people did not operate with money. People used barter, you give me a fruit or a manioc . . . I give you a fish. More favors, you see. Barter always functioned and still functions today. And he gave things to the people so that they would give him wood. He began constructing a bongo. The difficulty was with his language, but he could still communicate with the people. But they say he did not talk much to the people. He was a little bit serious and angry. People feared him a little. So, he built his bongo, loaded his box, and came to live on the island.

The people would fish near the island, and he remained living there. He was not very friendly. He was always near to his box. He had the bongo to fish with and would occasionally go to the village to get fresh water and other things he needed. And time passed like that, months, years, until one day the foreigner disappeared . . . disappeared completely. The people arrived one day. They could not find him. He disappeared, but the people did not think much of that. They began thinking about the box. "What could he have in it?" And the people looked all over the island. Imagine. What did they do? Looked in the sand, looked near the rocks. They didn't find the remains of the foreigner or the box. Nothing, nothing. Okay, so years passed. The years passed, passed, passed. And people gave him the nickname *Barbudazo* because he had a big beard. Barbudazo, Barbudazo, the gringo, the gringo. So, after some sixty, eighty years, people started to see a little bit more technology. People continued fish-ing and still fish now. People bought boats, motors, and they would go far to fish . . . further out. Sometimes there were ugly winds, rains, it was ugly, ugly. People did not want to go far out or they could not get back into port, so it was easier to fish here, close to the island. The people would come in their boats and set anchor here. Anchored here in front of the little beach, and here they would spend the night. Sometimes they would sleep two hours, three hours, it depended. And they would sleep. And the people started to hear someone swimming. They heard someone swimming from the beach [on the island] to the boat. All of them asleep. Suddenly, somebody began to moan . . . "mmmm-mmm, let me go, let me go, let me go." And sometimes someone would make a noise, "traaaaa," and they would wake [up]. The person who was overwhelmed would say, "It is a large gringo, it is a bearded one crushing me, he wouldn't let me move, like he wanted to suffocate me. He wanted me to leave." So, people came to know him as the Gringo Barbudazo. But the people said, "It is a nightmare, just a nightmare." They did not believe it very much. Then it happened to other boats, the same thing. The same thing happened to all of them, the same, the same. So, the story is that, shoot, it is said that he could have a treasure inside [the box]. His spirit thinks that we will rob him maybe, no? That is what the people believe.

So, he is there, and the box is somewhere. His treasure. The people think it is his treasure. Things of him and his family. It could be beneath the beach. Why doesn't his spirit rest in peace? Why does he come to bother the boats? Imagine. It is because he has something important. When they come at night and he arrives swimming, he arrives angry and climbs into the boat and wakes them. He does not allow anyone to sleep.

The story of the phantom presents numerous insights into themes that are prominent in this book. In thinking about the story, I am left with more questions than answers. However, it is worth presenting some of those themes here. One of the first things that stands out is the distinction made between local residents and the phantom. The phantom is clearly a foreigner, and more than that, he is a gringo. In all my conversations with residents, he has been described as tall, robust, light-skinned, light-eyed, and having a large beard that is light in color. He is a gringo. The recognition of difference with regard to the phantom and community residents relates well to the colonial history of Salango. Spanish contact with the community occurred in the 1520s, and the local culture was radically transformed as a consequence. Perhaps the phantom is a contemporary manifestation of the legacy of Spanish contact and colonialism in much the same way the highland Andean bogeyman known as the *pishtaco* represents the historical relationship between Native groups and the European outsiders. For Weismantel (2000:408) the pishtaco "crystallizes the collective wisdom of a community of color about the nature of whiteness." To be white, a gringo, is to be dominant, exploitive, mistrusted, and feared. Moreover, in the case of the pishtaco, rape and murder are defining features, and the pishtaco is a symbol of the domination and cultural transformation imposed by the Spanish.

While the phantom of Salango is not the same as the pishtaco, he shares the same values, the most significant of which are fear and distrust.

An alternative reading of the story of the phantom emphasizes the economic elements. In Diego's telling he makes multiple references to economic practices and interactions. He specifically references a system of barter as preceding the arrival of the phantom and the phantom using currency in his economic interactions with locals. According to Wolf's (1955) classic work on peasantry in Latin America, the corporate peasant community is defined by a level of social cohesion and interaction that represents a single sub-culture: the peasantry. Moreover, "The corporate community emphasizes resistance to influences from without which might threaten its integrity [and] frowns on individual accumulation and display of wealth and strives to reduce the effects of such accumulation on the communal structure. It resists reshaping of relationships; it defends the traditional equilibrium" (Wolf 1955:462). In addition to these characteristics, the corporate community is also subsistence-based and communal, and most economic production occurs within the community. From Wolf's perspective, the phantom can be read as a threat to the traditional economy of Salango or at least as a symbol of the threat outsiders pose to the corporate community structure. I am not suggesting that Salango is currently organized as a corporate community but that it likely was a few generations ago, at the time the bearded foreigner came to the village. An alternative yet related reading is that the phantom is an admonisher of the perils of capitalist growth and a shift from small-scale fishing to the more technologically involved and resource-exploitive fishing that began in the 1960s.

A final interpretation of the phantom is that it is a symbolic manifestation of the perils of the ocean. Fear of the phantom results in fishermen being aware of their surroundings and conscious of the omnipresent dangers, in a manner corresponding to P. Cohen's (1969) suggestion that myths deal with universal themes, including preoccupations with danger.

While I have no single definitive interpretation of the story of the phantom, I think it best to recognize that it likely encompasses components of all the themes outlined above. The phantom does not represent a single thing to any one individual but is instead multi-vocal in its meanings. As I elaborate in forthcoming chapters, the phantom may even extend beyond the interpretations discussed thus far.

Once fishermen say goodbye to their families, they make their way onto the beach. The men walk through the soft sand toward the various bongos. Each bongo is manned by an entire crew, which can consist of as many as eight individuals. The flat-bottomed bongos, which measure between 3 meters and

4 meters in length, are dragged painstakingly across the sand to where land meets ocean. *Pomas* (plastic tanks ranging in size from 3 to 10 gallons) full of diesel fuel are loaded into each bongo. With pant legs rolled up to avoid getting wet, the men scurry to climb into the bongos. When all but one person is onboard, the bongo is pushed into deeper water. The timing needs to be impeccable or the bongo will meet the crashing surf and either be tossed skyward and capsize or be consumed by the oncoming waves. I have experienced this painful connection with the ocean on more than one occasion, my body thrown from the bongo and driven onto the ocean floor. Unlike myself, local residents are experts, and years of experience have taught them the exact moment to approach the oncoming waves. Once the timing is perfect, the man at the stern gives one last push and one of the men in the bongo begins paddling furiously. The other men huddle close together as the bongo meets the first wave. It usually rolls effortlessly over the wave and out to the bay.

The men joke and laugh as the bongo glides gracefully across the smooth surface of the bay. Once they arrive at the moored chinchorrero, the men scramble to unload the fuel and themselves from the bongo. After all the men have made their way onto the chinchorrero, the bongo is tied to a main line connected to the chinchorrero's winch. The bongo is then hoisted onto the stern of the chinchorrero, where it will ride piggyback until it is time to drop the nets. By this time the sun is receding to the west, and daylight will soon be gone. The men usually spend the first few minutes aboard getting the boat prepared for the night's work. After that the men settle into conversation and eating. The chinchorrero rolls over the waves as the sun sets beyond the horizon. As the sky turns to darkness, the fishermen settle in for the night. Sleeping accommodations on the chinchorreros vary depending on the size of the boat and the money spent on luxuries such as foam mattresses and bunks. In many cases the crew is forced to sleep on the deck. Individuals huddle together and share in conversation before they drift off to sleep to the gentle rolling of the waves and the steady rumble of the engine.

The trip can last for as many as three or four hours before the boat reaches its destination. Upon arrival at the fishing grounds, the practice of using a light to locate the fish commences. One member of the crew climbs to the front of the boat and begins shining the light while looking intently at the surface of the ocean to spot the reflection. Once the fish are located, the action begins. The *capitán* alerts the crew, and the men awake without hesitation. They rush to pull their clothes off to avoid getting wet. Some of the men have raincoats or rain pants, but most are in shorts and T-shirts. They scramble about the boat in complete darkness as they ready the net.

The bongo is released off the back of the chinchorrero once everyone is in position. The dangerous job of manning the bongo in the turbulent water is most often given to the youngest member of the crew. His job is to maintain the position of the net as it enters the water from the back of the chinchorrero. Once the bongo is in the water the capitán engages the engine, pushing the chinchorrero ahead. The bongo and its young passenger are left behind in the darkness. The chinchorrero circles around in a wide loop until it once again meets the bongo. At this point the net is set, and the schooling fish are entrapped in the large circle it forms.

The men hustle to begin the process of pulling in the net. An onboard winch is used to pull the net and catch to the surface. Once the net is completely pulled in, except for the receptacle end, it is pinned between the chinchorrero and the bongo. The men begin quickly removing the fish with the use of a *gaveta*.[7] The fish are either thrown onto the deck or into the below-deck storage holds. After all the fish are removed and the net is secured on the deck, the bongo is pulled in and situated on top of the net. The men hustle back to the chinchorrero's cabin and exchange their wet clothing for the dry clothes they removed prior to dropping the net. They then resume their positions in the cabin and fall fast asleep for the return to Salango.

Mornings in Salango mark the dawn of a new day and the prospects of a successful catch. The community awakes at sunrise, and people leave their homes and walk the dirt streets to the beach. Women and children stand along the malecón while dogs run along the beach in anticipation of the arriving boats. Men greet each other with firm handshakes or with an extended clenched fist to indicate that their hands are unclean. When this is the case, the individual with clean hands grabs the forearm attached to the unclean hand. It is something akin to the now popular "fist bump" in the United States but was commonplace in coastal Ecuador long before the fist-bump gained appeal. The morning is a time for casual conversation between friends and family members.

As the early hours of the morning pass, the chinchorreros lumber past the island and into the bay. The timing of the arrival depends on the distance traveled by each boat and the success of the catch. The majority of Salango's chinchorreros work the waters to the south of the village, with some going as far as the Isla de la Plata, approximately 25 miles northwest of Salango, or Bajo Copéz, approximately 35 miles to the south. As the boats make the turn around the island or cut through the channel that separates the island from the mainland, the crowd begins to move to the beach.

Camionetas and larger diesel-powered camiones begin to arrive. They are contacted directly by the fishermen or by *comerciantes* who act as middlemen

FIGURE 2.5. *People gather at the beach in the morning.*

arranging the sale of the catch. Some of the trucks are owned by local fishermen while others are hired by the owner of the chinchorrero to transport the fish to market, either nearby Puerto López or one of Ecuador's two largest port cities, Manta and Guayaquil. Although not a direct part of fishing activities, women do play a prominent role in the local fishing economy. It is most frequently the wives of boat owners who keep accounts in small journals and who can be seen noting precisely the daily catch with amounts, weights, buyer and seller, and all other relevant information. The women keep a close eye on the activities and maintain meticulous records. Similarly, the wives of divers also play an important part in recordkeeping and maintaining the accounts of the daily harvest.

The sense of community that is generated through economic practice develops from the social relationships that form an intricate part of the daily interactions associated with making a living in Salango. While economic practice in Salango is market-based (e.g., based on profit and accumulation), it also exhibits relations that are representative of a community realm of interaction. For Gudeman, the distinction between market and community realms has

FIGURE 2.6. *The daily catch is sorted.*

to do with the intimacy of interactions and the role of relationships in the exchange. Whereas the "market realm revolves about short-term material relationships that are undertaken *for the sake of* achieving a project or securing a good . . . material goods are exchanged through relationships *kept for their own sake*" in the communal realm (Gudeman 2001:10, original emphasis). This is not to suggest that community exchanges exist without expectation of return; instead, it refers to the social substance of interactions. Taking this a step further and building on Sahlins's (1972) discussion of reciprocity, economic interactions have the capacity to create a sense of community. A brief example will illustrate this point.

At the same time trucks are loaded with fish to go to market, with the goal of accumulating wealth, fish are also shared with friends, family members, and onlookers. Elderly members of the village are taken care of through the practice of gifting a few fish. The recipients of such gifts are often individuals who have little to no means of providing for themselves and who lack family support or extended networks of kin. The providing of a gift is a form of reciprocity that represents close social relations and serves as "an expression of community" (Gudeman 2001:86). The giving of fish falls near the extreme end of Sahlins's model of reciprocity where the social aspect of the interaction represses the material aspect, and debts are not calculated (Sahlins 1972). This does not mean the exchange is without an obligation in return, but the return is not calculated with respect to "time, quality, or quantity" (Sahlins 1972:194). Communal exchanges function to create community, and community is an intrinsic value that develops from shared experience and understanding. The community realm and the market realm are not mutually exclusive, and witnessing a morning on the beach in Salango lends credibility to this statement.

The previously addressed relations, along with the majority of economic interactions in Salango, are predicated on a specific set of interactions not only with other individuals but also with the environment. Following the perspective put forth by Tsing (2001), the natural environment and all it encompasses (e.g., mountains, rivers, valleys, trees) can be conceived of as "actors" in human histories where nature is not an objective entity but a part of human experience (Narotzky 1997). It is through this connection to nature that local residents establish a sense of collective identity.

A brief example of the role of the environment in the formation of identity comes from a conversation I had with local community officials during my first time in the field in 2002. I met with Mauricio and Marta at the *casa comunal*. The initial reason for my visit was to speak with them about economic practices in the community. I was familiar with the importance of the local fishing and diving economies, but I was less clear on the significance of land use in Salango. From what little I could glean at that time, it appeared to me that despite the fact that the community possessed a significant amount of land, the majority of it was either fallow or overgrown by forest. I asked Mauricio about this observation. His response was direct: "The people look over there [to the Pacific Ocean] and not over there [toward the land] . . . we are a fishing village and the people live for fishing." For Mauricio, the role of the Pacific Ocean in the lives of the people of Salango was not to be ignored. The ocean is a part of

FIGURE 2.7. *Don Orlando*

daily life. The dense tropical air smells of salt, and the sound of waves reaching the shore is a constant reminder of peoples' relationship to the natural environment. Economic livelihoods drawn from the ocean permeate daily life.

A song written and performed by local resident don Orlando highlights the significance of landscape and identity. The song was performed for me on numerous occasions prior to don Orlando's passing in 2006, and it is still sung by his sons and is also known well and regarded highly by most members of the community. It is a local anthem of sorts, and for years a copy of the song hung on the wall of the family restaurant—the same restaurant where I first met Diego early in my research.

How beautiful and lovely are your beaches	*Que hermosa y bella que son tus playas*
Adorned by the ocean	*Adornados por el mar*
There exists a virtuous island	*Allí existe una isla virtuosa la que*
That we should remember	*Por ella debemos recordar*
And very happy I sing to you about my Salango	*Y muy alegre le canto a mi Salango*

Because I am a child of my native village	*Porque soy hijo de mi pueblo natal*
And very happy I sing to you about my Salango	*Y muy alegre le canto a mi Salango*
Because I am a child of my native village	*Porque soy hijo de mi pueblo natal*
The union of fisherman	*El sindicato de pescadores*
Was formed in reality	*Fue formado en realidad*
By expert Salangueños	*Por expertos Salangüenses*
That are children of this place	*Que son hijos de este lugar*
Salango loved port	*Salango puerto querido*
The most beautiful of Manabí	*El más hermoso de Manabí*
There are women of beauty	*Hay belleza de mujeres*
Like flowers in its garden	*Como flores en su jardín*
And with pride I sing to you about my little village	*Y con orgullo le canto de mi pueblito*
Beautiful Salango where I was born	*Salango lindo donde yo nací*
And with pride I sing to you about my village	*Con orgullo le canto a mi pueblo*
So that you have a memory of me	*Para que tenga recuerdo de mí*
And Ayampe, San Vicente, and Puerto Rico	*Y Ayampe, San Vicente, y Puerto Rico*
Are horticultural zones of here	*Son recintos productores de aquí*
And they are loved by my land Salango	*Y son queridos de mi tierra de Salango*
And as a brother I love them the same	*Y como hermano lo quiero yo así*
For the sultan of coffee that is produced in Manabí	*Por la sultana de café, la que produce en Manabí*
(They all love her because she is very pretty, my Ecuador)	*(Todos le quieren con amor por que es muy lindo mi Ecuador)*

The song reflects on various themes presented throughout this chapter. It references the connection and pride residents feel about their community and the cognitive links they make among identity, economic practice, and the natural environment. The song begins by noting prominent natural elements that make up the village and that serve as foundations for shared experiences and collective memory: the beach, the ocean, and the island. The song then transitions to express the sense of pride felt in being a child of the village. This same sense of pride and identity is a common identity referent, as community members frequently refer to themselves as *hijos del pueblo* (children of the village). The song then shifts to an explicit reference to the local fishing industry before establishing connections between Salango and outlying horticultural communities that form part of the broader southern Manabí region. The final lines of the song reference the history of coffee production and situate Salango within Ecuador. Conforming to Gudeman's (2001) discussion of community, the song identifies economic practice as a prominent component of local identity. As the song illustrates, economic activity provides a foundation for contemporary community identity, an identity that is crafted through shared experience and understanding. While my approach is largely materialistic, I in no way argue that contemporary notions of community identity are solely the result of the material conditions present in Salango. Instead, I suggest that economic practice and the embodiment of shared experience have a strong influence on localized conceptions of community identity.

In chapter 3 I focus on another foundational component on which contemporary community identity is grounded. I contend that both contemporary economic practices as well as the rich prehistory of Salango and the surrounding region serve as important points of emphasis in the articulation of community identity. As illustrated in chapter 3, economic practice, inasmuch as it is tied to the natural environment and the economic base of the Pacific Ocean, illustrates a degree of cultural continuity from the past to the present.

NOTES

1. A 1992 study conducted by the New York City Department of City Planning and cited in the *New York Times* (September 2, 1993, B1) indicates that Ecuadorians made up the largest number of undocumented immigrants in New York City during the study year. Jokisch and Pribilsky (2002) estimate that over 250,000 Ecuadorians emigrated between 1999 and 2000.

2. The economic decline of the 1990s can in part be attributed to the political instability and corruption that were endemic in Ecuador during that period.

3. The beach seines that were used in my early years of fieldwork were not used in the ocean but instead in a small estuary that would form where the river met the ocean. The water would pool and trap small fish and shrimp that would be harvested using a modified beach seine net.

4. Negra, albacora, and bonito are all members of the tuna family. In my early years of fieldwork, they were fairly common, and on occasion the local chinchorreros would catch tons of albacora in a single night of fishing. Such catches are now extremely rare.

5. The quintal is a standard unit of measure used throughout Manabí and refers to a unit of 100 pounds. Most corvina (weakfish) weigh 5 to 10 pounds, with extremely large fish being upward of 20 pounds.

6. Guato is the local name for Goliath Grouper. As the name implies, the fish are immense in size and can grow to well over 400 pounds. They are almost always caught by divers who spear them when diving among deep water rocky outcrops.

7. A gaveta is a plastic bin akin to a recycling bin. It is used to transport fish and is also used as a unit of measurement. For example, a catch may be quantified as being 50 gavetas.

3

Encountering the Past

Archaeology, Materiality, and the Foundations of Identity

According to geographer Brian Osborne, "The past is not *preserved*, but is *socially constructed* through its representation in such memory-machines as archives, museums, national chronicles, school curricula, monuments, and public displays" (Osborne 2006:152). While a great deal of the social construction of the past is associated with narratives on national identity (see Benavides 2008; Díaz-Andreu and Champion 2015; Kohl and Faucett 1995), the use of the past to shape alternative narratives about identity is becoming increasingly recognized by scholars (see Benavides 2011; Rowe 2012; Silverman 2006). Such accounts re-envision the past as locally grounded and site-specific while at the same time often fostering localized claims to identity. Benavides (2011:258) suggests that a critical part of this process is establishing claims about the past that emphasize "a first-person narrative" in which references to the archaeological record are no longer couched in terms of prominent civilizations of the past and achievements that are temporally and symbolically removed from the present but are referenced in terms of contributions made by "we Indians" and "our ancestors."

Manuel has a small hutch in the living room of his home. Photos, gifts from graduations and baptisms, and photo albums adorn the hutch along with *Spondylus* shells, small pot sherds, and a few more elaborate pieces of ceramic vessels. The most elaborate is the neck of a vessel containing a face that is

DOI: 10.5876/9781607327608.c003

typical of the Manteño period. The Manteño inhabited the region of southern Manabí province from AD 800 until Spanish contact in the early sixteenth century (Harris et al. 2004; Martínez, Graber, and Harris 2006), and Manteño artifacts are well-known throughout the region and are commonly found during construction projects. In fact, in 2014 multiple Manteño burial vessels were encountered during excavation for sewer lines in Salango.

Archaeologists have long paid attention to the Manteño culture. To residents of Salango and surrounding communities, the Manteño represent a clear link to the region's Indigenous prehistory (Bauer 2008, 2014; Bauer and Lunniss 2010). Throughout my time in Salango, it became clear to me that archaeology and the past provide contributions to local understandings of identity in the present. In this chapter I focus on the material (archaeological) connections that link residents to the Indigenous past, with special attention paid to *Spondylus* and its importance for contemporary residents of Salango. I also address contemporary expressions of indigeneity through an analysis of the ritual performance of the annual balsa festival held in Salango every October 12 and the twentieth anniversary celebration of Salango's museum.

Artifacts like those exhibited in Manuel's living room are not only representations of the rich prehistory of Salango; they also form a foundation for claims about contemporary local identity (Bauer 2014). The archaeology of coastal Ecuador has been well documented by numerous scholars, with an early contribution coming in the form of Meggers's (1966) text, *Ecuador*. That work marks the growth of a developing interest in coastal Ecuadorian archaeology. Subsequent work by scholars including Currie (1995), Harris and colleagues (2004), Lunniss (2001, 2008), Marcos (1986), Martin (2007, 2009), Martínez (1997), Martínez and colleagues (2006), Masucci (1995), McEwan (2003), McEwan and colleagues (2006), and Norton (1986), among others, has provided significant insights into the pre-Columbian cultural complexity of the south-central Ecuadorian coast; and since Meggers's early work, a significant amount of research has been conducted in and around Salango.

Archaeological investigations in southern Manabí began in the late 1970s. Most notably, archaeologist Presley Norton began research in the community of Salango and continued work there until the 1980s. Norton's work represents the longest and most extensive archaeological research project conducted in Ecuador. An analysis of the excavated materials continues to this day. The culmination of Norton's work was the establishment of the community museum in 1987. Norton's memory lives on not only in the museum but also in resident recollections of his time in the community and his employment of numerous community residents who aided in the archaeological excavations.

The museum at Salango is located at the north end of town, along the beachfront. It is unique in Ecuador, as it is the only museum that is housed, albeit partially, in a turn-of-the-century hacienda home; it is also one of the few existing original hacienda homes found along the Ecuadorian coast. The main portion of the museum contains a single room covered by a steep conical roof that was once covered in traditional palm fronds which have more recently been replaced with metal sheeting. The interior of the museum is constructed with local hardwoods and contains numerous glass cases that house hundreds of artifacts uncovered during the excavations of Norton and his field crew. A time line along the east wall details the occupations of the region, beginning with the *Valdivia* 5,000 years ago and ending with the Manteño in the 1520s. In addition to the extensive display of artifacts, there is a model of a wooden raft that represents the type of sailing vessel used by the Manteño at the time of Spanish conquest. A final component of the museum is a large display of *Spondylus* artifacts and shells that also contains a photograph of a contemporary *Spondylus* diver. The display establishes a connection between the archaeological artifacts housed in the museum and the contemporary residents of Salango.

Spondylus, a genus of marine bivalve that can be found in tropical waters the world over, is of great importance to the residents of Salango and to the broader coastal region because it is the only significant tangible link to the pre-Columbian past. As such, *Spondylus* is the most prominent material marker associated with Salango (Bauer 2007b). The two species of *Spondylus* native to the waters off the coast of Ecuador are *Spondylus princeps* and *Spondylus calcifer,* and both species have captured the imagination of archaeologists and locals alike. Research on the pre-Columbian use of *Spondylus* suggests its importance as both a trade item (Harris et al. 2004; Marcos 1986; Masucci 1995; Norton 1986) and an item of ceremonial/ritual significance (Blower 1995; Currie 1995; Marcos 1986; Martin 2001; Paulsen 1974; Rostworowski and Morris 1999; Sandweiss 1999; Shimada 1999). Evidence of the importance of *Spondylus* is presented in the sixteenth-century Quechua language text known as *The Huarochirí Manuscript* (Salomon and Urioste 1991). The manuscript presents Indigenous beliefs and cosmology with a focus on *huacas* (locations of ritual significance believed to be inhabited by gods or spirits) and the religious cults associated with them. *Spondylus* is referenced throughout the text as representing a sacred offering to the huacas, and numerous scholars cite *Spondylus* as an offertory item associated with water-giving deities and agricultural and fishing productivity (see Rostworowski and Morris 1999; Shimada 1999 for more detail). There is also strong archaeological evidence to support the contention

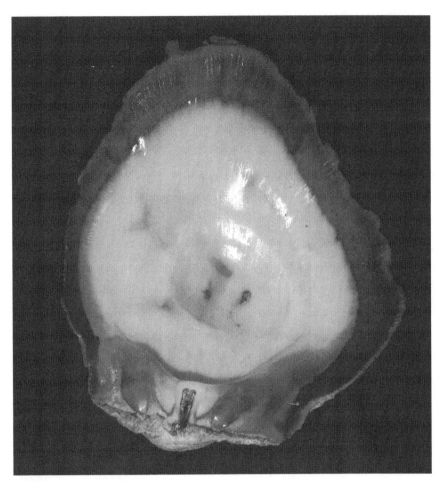

FIGURE 3.1. *Spondylus princeps*

that *Spondylus* was associated with elite status. Carter and Helmer (2015) make note of this in their detailed discussion of pre-Columbian regional identity and ornaments, while Shimada (1999) and Graber and Jastremski (2009) also argue for the political importance of *Spondylus* as a symbol of power and prestige.

Archaeological evidence from sites in and around Salango indicates that the region was likely home to workshops used in the production of worked *Spondylus* (Graber and Jastremski 2009; Harris et al. 2004; Norton, Lunniss, and Nayling 1983; Paulsen 1974), and there is general recognition by archaeologists that coastal Ecuador was a center for *Spondylus* procurement and long-distance trade (Rostworowski and Morris 1999; Shimada 1999; Villamarín and Villamarín 1999). As anecdotal evidence of the importance of *Spondylus*, one can easily find small pieces of *Spondylus* shell scattered along the beach at Salango. The fragments wash in with the tide and litter the south end of the beach. I have collected these small pieces on numerous occasions and rarely gave much thought to them until recently. What appears odd is why the fragments would be found in such large quantities, since today *Spondylus* is not processed in the ocean or at the beach but instead at the homes of local residents. Moreover, most shells that are harvested by divers who live in Salango are kept intact and are only broken into smaller pieces by the few artisans currently living in Salango. The explanation, then, must be that the fragments that wash in with the tide are likely from past use, perhaps dating as far back as the Manteño.

BENEATH THE SURFACE

One afternoon Manuel and I were working in the backyard of his family home. Manuel built his home on a small lot near the center of town, just down the street from the Catholic Church. At the time, the home had one bedroom as well as a small living room that adjoined the kitchen and a single bathroom. Manuel had a young son and a second child on the way, and he had asked me to help with some work in the backyard. His lot backs up to that of his neighbor, and there was no real separation between the two. Manuel wished to construct a small fence made from old pieces of bamboo and scrap wood as well as some abandoned fishing nets he had piled next to the house. The plan was to sink the posts into the ground and then stretch the netting across them. This, it was hoped, would keep Manuel's chickens in and the neighbor's chickens out.

The sun was hot, but an afternoon rain threatened as dark clouds moved in slowly from the hills to the east. We worked diligently to sink each post and then to stretch the net and secure it with nails taken from a collection of used nails Manuel housed in a plastic jug stashed away near his workbench. The final step to complete the fence was to place stones along the net at the point where it met the ground. The stones, it was hoped, would keep the chickens from getting under the net and would also keep the net in place. "What do you think about planting some banana trees along the fence?" I asked Manuel. "Seems like a good idea," he responded. "We can get some young ones from the front." The front of the house was home to a fairly large banana tree that had numerous new offspring growing at its base. The wonderful thing about bananas is that they reproduce very quickly and transplanting them is quite easy.

Manuel grabbed his machete and with a downward stabbing motion began plunging it into the soft sandy soil at the base of some of the young plants. The soil turned over easily, and the soft roots were cut with a few brisk swings of the machete. "We are ready," commented Manuel. We walked back to the fence line as the clouds grew increasingly imposing. "Where should we put them?" he asked. I pointed to a few spots I thought would be good, and each of us began digging with the machetes we had in hand. The holes did not need to be big, just big enough for the root bundle to fit, and the soil came up easily. The only exception was when I hit something about 15 centimeters below that made my machete bow in my hand as a result of the downward pressure I imposed on the blade. "There is something here," I said to Manuel as I dug more quickly. It did not take long until I unearthed a *Spondylus* shell. It was weathered from its time buried beneath the soil and there was no way to know just how old it was, but it certainly had been there for a long time, and it provided evidence of earlier occupation. Manuel and I walked over to the cistern and began to rinse off the shell. As the dirt disappeared, the faded orange color of the *Spondylus* was revealed. A more thorough scrubbing of the shell exposed the intricacies of the shell's exterior. After a few photos, the shell would eventually be placed on the small hutch in Manuel's living room.

Finds like the *Spondylus* shell are commonplace in Salango; indeed, it is not inaccurate to suggest that the past lies shallowly beneath the surface of the community. A trip to the property of Manuel's *suegro* (father-in-law) illustrates this reality. Manuel maintains a close political relationship with his suegro, and when Manuel was just starting out, he would often borrow his suegro's *fibra* to go fishing so he could support his family. To foster the relationship, Manuel would often accompany don Jorge to his land to clear weeds and lend a hand in the daily labor. Don Jorge's land is situated on a high hill overlooking the community and the bay. One of the most interesting features of the property is that it is littered with pottery sherds. The sherds vary in shape and size, but most are of Manteño origin and are exposed because of frequent rains. I asked don Jorge about the sherds and he explained, "They have always been here, and sometimes large pieces of ceramic or stone are found." He did not go into great detail, perhaps because to him the existence of the pottery was nothing out of the ordinary. In fact, don Jorge went about his own business, walking the plot and inspecting his old *cabaña* while Manuel and I surveyed the ground for sherds. We examined a few and noted the intricate designs, but after a short time the novelty wore off, and the gathered sherds were tossed back onto the ground.

Figure 3.2. *View from the hill on don Jorge's property*

More striking than the archaeological material present on the surface of don Jorge's land is the view that looks out over the bay. One could imagine the importance of this hilltop at the time of Manteño occupation and how it possibly served as a lookout point. On a clear day the Isla de la Plata can be seen; there is also a clear vantage point to Isla Salango to the south, an island many Salangueños claim had ceremonial significance during the Manteño period. There is also a clear line of sight to the north, beyond the rocky point that marks the edge of the bay. The view from the hill would have been advantageous for keeping tabs on incoming and outgoing trading vessels as well as monitoring movements in the community below. This location and others throughout Salango inspired my interest in how the past impacts the present and how the people of Salango understand their own (pre)history.

During the spring of 2005, I made a trip to Salango with an archaeologist friend. He had done work in Guatemala and Belize and asked to accompany me to Ecuador so he could get to know the area where I conduct research. I told him about the wealth of archaeological material but the veritable lack of any significant monumental structures similar to those representative of the Maya or Inca. We visited the museum in Salango and the nearby museums in Agua Blanca and Valdivia and, as chance would have it, trenches were being dug throughout Salango to put in tubing for water. The trenches ran along the side of the main roadways through town and were a meter or so deep and about 80 centimeters wide. The soil was piled up along the edges of the trenches, and a quick glance down revealed pottery sherds, bits of shell, and occasional pieces of bone.

A few days later we were invited to eat at the home of my compadre Pedro. He and his wife, Carolina, were living in a small home along one of the main streets of Salango. The home was rented from a family member who had an adjoining house. We sat under a thatched awning that protected the front porch from the midday sun. The heat was intense, and the shade provided valuable relief. Pedro greeted us with a big smile. "Compa, how are you? What sun! You guys are sweating," he said with a laugh. Carolina was in the kitchen cooking. It was hard to see her through the window because of the relative darkness inside compared to the intense sunlight on the outside. "Hola, compa! The food will be ready soon," she yelled from the kitchen. Pedro and Carolina have always been very endearing people, as are most in Salango, and they have a wonderful habit of feeding me the most delicious meals. On this occasion Carolina had prepared one of her specialties, lobster in garlic sauce with a side of coconut rice, fried plantains, and salad. "Have a seat, compa," Pedro exclaimed as he pulled out the plastic chairs from the matching plastic table on the front porch. "I am going to get a cola," he said, removing some coins from his pocket. He then hustled two doors down to a *tienda* that sells drinks, snacks, toiletries, and a few other necessities. "What do you think about the holes [trenches]?" I asked when he returned. In a half-joking manner with a wry smile, as is common for Pedro, he exclaimed, "These holes are everywhere; it is a mess!" For Pedro, the trenches were obviously an inconvenience as they needed to be jumped over or a wooden plank needed to be placed across them to get out of the front of the house and into the street. "They have been working on them for a long time, but they say we are going to have water. Each house will have it, and you will just have to turn the key [nozzle]."

The access to water was a tangible sign of progress. No longer would residents have to wait for a tanker truck to come to fill up the cistern. The water would literally be at one's fingertips. It was a promise that would represent Salango's path toward development, just as electricity, telephone service, and the main coastal highway had done in the past. It was one more step toward development and something that at the time was eagerly anticipated by most community residents. However, the irony of such progress is that the past was unearthed as a consequence of the trenches being dug. This was nothing new to the people of Salango but simply confirmed what they already knew about the region's deep prehistory and its presence in their daily routines.

Construction projects in Salango frequently result in residents encountering the past with the strike of a shovel. While these are in no way formal archaeological excavations, they are informed by what locals know about the archaeological record, and it is common for residents to seek out archaeologists to provide information on the backyard finds. Manuel shared one such find with me. I remember vividly the excitement on Manuel's face when he explained how he found a piece of a ceramic vessel with the form of a Manteño face. Manuel received a truckload of dirt to fill in his backyard, and the dirt was dumped at the front of his home: "I went out to work, and the first time I put the shovel in the soil I hit something. I thought it was a rock at first, and I reached in to pull it out. It was not a rock; it was a ceramic!" The piece is not complete, but it has the characteristic features of Manteño ceramics, including the prominent nose most strongly associated with ceramics from the Manteño period and which is also quite characteristic of many local residents. As I illustrate later in this chapter, the significance of the Manteño nose extends well beyond the archaeological record.[1]

For residents of Salango, the importance of the archaeological record is not just a part of daily life but is bolstered by the contemporary material importance of *Spondylus*. I initially became aware of *Spondylus* during my first trip to Salango and my encounter with Diego. At that time he showed me one of the largest *Spondylus* shells I have ever seen, and he shared a brief summary of the shell's significance: "Salango is the cradle of *Spondylus*. They [archaeologists] say it was the food of the gods and that our ancestors used it as money." "How do you get it?" I asked. "I am a diver. My brothers are also divers. You can find *Spondylus* near the island . . . where there are rocks," Diego explained with pride. I have found that this same sense of pride is exhibited by most divers and artisans who work with *Spondylus*, and in subsequent trips to Salango I continued to develop my curiosity about *Spondylus* as well as my relationships with local divers and artisans.

Manuel is one of the few remaining *Spondylus* artisans in Salango. When I first began my research, a handful of artisans were living in the community, some more skilled than others; but the decline of *Spondylus* and government restrictions prohibiting the harvesting of the shell have resulted in a reduction in *Spondylus* artisanship. Early in my time in Salango, when Manuel was transitioning from his parents' home to his own home, he had a small work bench in the backyard of his parents' home. It was there that Manuel would fashion jewelry from *Spondylus* and mother of pearl. "How did you learn?" I once asked Manuel. He explained that his grandfather used to work with *Spondylus*, and as a young boy he would watch, and he slowly developed the skill through experimentation and creativity (Bauer 2007b).

The process of working *Spondylus* is time- and labor-intensive. The shell is extremely hard, and hours can be spent grinding down a shell to create the desired design. Manuel mostly makes small pendants for use on necklaces or

FIGURE 3.3. *Manuel working in his workshop while his young son watches.*

earrings, and he used to make beads for necklaces. Manuel predominantly sells to tourists, most of whom are attracted to *Spondylus* and the story behind it. Manuel and other artisans are well versed at relaying an abridged history of the Manteño and Salango with an emphasis on *Spondylus.* They talk about how it dates back 5,000 years and how it was the "food of the gods" and important for long-distance trade prior to the arrival of the Spanish. Even with this sales pitch, few tourists buy the more expensive jewelry made from the shells, and most opt for trinkets that relate to their own experiences visiting coastal Ecuador. The items include small pendants fashioned in the form of surfboards, fish, and whale tails that can be linked directly to tourist activities such as surfing, sport fishing, and whale watching. The designs are directly influenced by the growing tourist market and the need to create inexpensive pieces that cater to tourists' desire to connect with their experiences. As noted by García Canclini, the symbolic meaning associated with Native arts and crafts shifts when such items are marketed for tourists and "there is a prevalence of the cultural (aesthetic) value of tourists, who inscribe it within their own symbolic system, which is different from—and at times opposed to—the

Indian system" (García Canclini 1993:61–62). Manuel reported that tourists asked him for designs that related to their own experiences and symbolic frameworks. As such, the continued use of *Spondylus* fulfills a "demand for 'exotic' objects" desired by tourists while also serving to "fulfill certain functions within social reproduction" (García Canclini 1993:37–41). The concept of "social reproduction," also read as cultural reproduction, is of particular relevance to the case of Salango and *Spondylus* artisans. Working with *Spondylus* allows artisans to continue a practice, albeit in a modified form, that dates back nearly 5,000 years while also affording them the opportunity to take advantage of a growing tourist market (Bauer 2007b). The current focus on *Spondylus* represents a phenomenon Kistler (2014:79) refers to as "embodying the past." The basic premise is that value, pride, and prestige are achieved through maintaining occupational forms that are reflective of or related to an "original and authentic" past (Kistler 2014).

PERFORMING IDENTITY: SYMBOL AND MEANING

While the archaeological record and material and symbolic links to *Spondylus* serve to inform Salangueño identity on everyday occasions, more celebrated events reinforce and elaborate on local identity and claimed connections to the past. Two such events include the annual festival celebrating Indigenous heritage and Salango's ties to the ancestral Manteño population and the twentieth anniversary celebration of the local museum.

El Día de la Raza is celebrated each October 12 throughout Latin America. It corresponds with Columbus Day, or, alternatively, Indigenous Peoples' Day in the United States. The name literally translates to "the Day of the Race," and in various expressions it celebrates the birth of a unique Latin American identity that combines Spanish and Indigenous influences. The doctrine of "*la Raza*," as it is contemporarily known, was inspired by Latin America's colonial history and the mixing of Indigenous and Spanish populations, as related in chapter 2.

Early in my research I was told about *El Festival de la Balsa Manteña*, and during subsequent research trips I was able to witness and participate in the festival. The festival has been held each October 12 since 1992, although not in 2016, and it is a powerful reference to the region's pre-Columbian antiquity while also signifying the collective expression of identity and ancestry for the people of Salango. The Festival de la Balsa Manteña illustrates the complexity of ethnicity in Ecuador while also highlighting the importance of the past in the construction of ethnic identity. Moreover, the celebration reaffirms the prehistory of the region to emphasize collective identity and the relationship of residents to the past cultures of coastal Ecuador. As festivals are cultural mechanisms for expressing identity (Radcliffe 1990), a great deal can be gleaned from studying the balsa festival and its role in residents' lives. In particular, the festival provides insights into expressions of local identity and the politics of identity as related to prehistory and place. The festival is indicative of how general concepts and notions of identity are packaged into concrete expressions or self-representations at specific historical moments.

The year 2006 marked the fifteenth annual Festival de la Balsa Manteña. The festival was organized originally by a group of young men and women who collectively were part of the group CEDESA (*Centro Juvenil del Desarrollo de Salango* [Youth Center for the Development of Salango]). The group was started with the main goal of organizing an annual festival to be celebrated on El Día de la Raza. I spoke with the president of CEDESA, Mauricio, on the eve of the festival. Mauricio recounted the history of the festival and its auspicious beginning:

> The festival was initiated in 1992 . . . it was more or less September of 1992 when CONAIE [Confederation of Indigenous Nationalities of Ecuador] and other Latin American organizations prepared to celebrate 500 years of Indigenous resistance. Therefore, during that time, we saw with clear vision that they spoke more about Indigenous resistance than the arrival of Columbus and the Spanish to Latin America. So we said, "What can we do here on the coast since CONAIE has concentrated on preparing the highlands?" We thought that we should celebrate by remembering the last culture, the Manteño culture, who were encountered by the Spanish.

Preparation began on October 10, a mere two days before the festival was to begin. Leading up to this date, many people commented about the perceived lack of preparation for the festival. As I ate breakfast with Manuel and his family, the sounds coming from the radio caught my attention. The normal talk of national politics, regional and local candidates, and the upcoming elections was interrupted by a local news segment that promoted the festival. Familiar voices came over the radio as members of CEDESA and friends of mine, Hector and Andréa, began speaking of the importance of the festival and its meaning to the people of Salango: "The festival represents the past of Salango. It is a celebration of our history and the ancestral populations of Salango. Each day we are losing our cultural values. We need to recover our cultural identity . . . the identity of the coast . . . the identity of this region.

We are descendants of an ancient culture. The festival is a celebration of the ancient cultures of the coast and our ancestry."

Andréa's interview brings to light a number of significant features with reference to local understandings of ethnic identity. The most prominent feature of ethnic identity is that it is based on an asserted relationship to the ancestral populations of the region. As descendants of the pre-Columbian inhabitants of the southern Manabí coast, Salangueños claim a unique identity that is tied to the region's rich prehistory. The two claims of ancestry and history form the cornerstones of contemporary ethnic identity and exist beyond the realm of the festival, even though the festival is the most condensed and accessible expression of such identity.

Since its inception, the festival has been organized around a simple theme. It serves to commemorate community prehistory. Concomitantly, it exists as a manifestation of the unique cultural identity of Salango, an identity that is cultivated from the past. The festival also acts as a mechanism of resistance by celebrating the Día de la Raza, not as "an annual holiday commemorating the arrival of Columbus in the Americas" (Tilley 2005:60) but as an annual holiday celebrating the Indigenous past and the Indigenous present. During our conversation, Mauricio went on to share the following: "Why do we call it the Festival de la Balsa Manteña, and why do we hold the festival in here? It is generally said that the Manteño culture in Ecuador, archaeologically and anthropologically, consisted of four lords . . . during this time the primary site was inland, but Salango was the principal port. Therefore, they sailed from here. Also included in this is the chronicle that speaks of the balsa encountered [while] leaving the port of Salango."

The festival commemorates Salango's Indigenous past through the construction of a replica raft made of balsa wood. Members of CEDESA build the raft in the days preceding the festival. While the raft varies from year to year, it maintains a degree of continuity in its overall appearance. The raft is built using large balsa logs measuring from 4 meters to 7 meters in length. The logs are laid side by side, with the longest log in the center and the shorter logs on the outside. They are then hafted together using rope to form the base of the raft. The construction techniques used to make the raft are drawn from early Spanish historical accounts of native rafts encountered off the Ecuadorian coast. Once completed, the raft stays on the beach until the day of the festival.

Each year the festival is organized in a similar manner. The festival begins with a parade through the streets of town. People flock to the parade route to watch the festivities. Friends and family members greet one another, sharing pleasant conversation as they wait for the parade. Since this is a public occasion, most people are neatly dressed, as is common for virtually all important festivities. Men generally dress in pants and either neatly pressed button-down shirts or brightly colored T-shirts. In virtually all cases, even when shorts are worn, shirts are tucked in, and shoes, as opposed to the more common flip-flops, are worn. Women wear sundresses or pants and blouses. Children are usually dressed immaculately, and most of the young boys have their hair slicked back with gel. The scent of perfume fills the air as people congregate to watch the parade as it passes. The occasion is one of importance not only for the festival participants but for the community as a whole.

Parade participants include members of the community as well as invited participants from nearby towns and villages and guests from the *sierra*, the *oriente*, and abroad. Parade participants dress in various stylized costumes that represent their ethnic affiliation. Participants from Salango and nearby communities wear "Indigenous" costumes consisting of loincloths, body paint, and beaded headdresses. Participants from Esmeraldas don "traditional" Afro-Ecuadorian attire; the women wear brightly colored floral-patterned dresses, and the men wear brightly colored button-down shirts. Participants from the highlands wear clothing representing their native highland communities. At the conclusion of the parade, all of the participating groups as well as onlookers congregate on the beach.

Hundreds of observers gather on the malecón and the surrounding beach area while brightly clothed children scurry across the sand to find the optimal place for viewing the festivities. The entire village seems to be in attendance, as is the norm for community festivals in small-town Ecuador. Micro-buses from Quito and Guayaquil line the malecón as visitors from Ecuador's two largest cities arrive for the festival. Participating groups line the wall of the malecón, watching intently.

The blowing of a conch shell signifies the beginning of the festivities on the beach. Participants gather in the center of an area demarcated by rope. The boundaries separate the social spaces of participants and spectators while also symbolically demarcating past and present. The activities within the cordoned-off area represent the Indigenous past through the use of stylized costumes as well as explicit markers, including Manteño artifacts such as stone net weights and anchors. This stands in marked contrast to the onlookers, who wear pressed pants and T-shirts, tennis shoes, and baseball caps.

Throughout the introduction the crowd is welcomed as a brief commentary positions the contemporary community within the context of the past: "We are here to participate in a celebration of our ancestral roots . . . a community celebration of our race . . . to celebrate the cultural and natural wealth of

FIGURE 3.4. *Onlookers at the balsa festival*

our zone . . . long live our culture." Various symbols of indigeneity converge as invited shamans from Ecuador's highlands begin the ceremony by blessing participants. The use of highland Andean shamans signifies a symbolic connection to the Indigenous culture of Ecuador by way of attachment to a region considered the heart of Ecuadorian indigeneity while at the same time reinforcing notions of indigeneity on the coast, a region that has not traditionally been regarded as Indigenous. The shamans, wearing matching light cotton shirts and white trousers, surround a small fire built at the center of the performance area. Members of each participating group come forward to receive the ritual blessing that invokes native symbols. Divers from Salango, carrying *Spondylus* shells, are called forward. They are introduced as the "great divers of Salango," and reference is made to the "sacred shell" of *Spondylus*. The most notable use of native symbolism is in the form of offerings made to *pacha mama* (Mother Earth), a Kichwa term most strongly associated with Indigenous nationalities of Ecuador's highland and Amazonian regions that does not hold particular salience on the Ecuadorian coast. The invocation to pacha mama establishes and fortifies a link to indigeneity that is not present in the daily lives of Salangueños.

After the presentation of the shaman, the festival continues with the election of *la Señorita Manteña Bonita*. The fact that a beauty contest is associated with the festival is not surprising. Beauty pageants are a part of virtually every community festival held in Salango. However, given the theme of this festival, the pageant is a little different from most. Each of the participating groups has one or more representatives take part in the pageant. Ultimately, the young woman deemed to exhibit characteristics most representative of the Manteño culture is awarded the title "Señorita Manteña Bonita." By their very definition, the characteristics of the Manteño culture are rather elusive, since the culture was altered radically after the arrival of the Spanish in the sixteenth century; the fact that the pageant is concerned with choosing the individual who is most "Manteño-like" automatically means that certain contestants will be eliminated by virtue of their own ethnic background.

Judges for the pageant are chosen by the organizing committee. As a foreigner who is deeply familiar with the community and its members, I have been asked to judge beauty pageants in Salango on numerous occasions, and the Señorita Manteña Bonita was no exception. The criteria for judging were clear. Señorita Manteña Bonita should possess physical characteristics that are representative of the Manteño population that inhabited the region from AD 800 until the Spanish conquest in the early 1500s. This alone is difficult to assess. However, one thing that does make the decision a bit easier is the knowledge that a common phenotypical feature of the Manteño people was a prominent nose. Manteño ceramics, like the one displayed on Manuel's hutch, exhibit this feature, as do numerous people living in and around Salango. The "typical" Manteño nose is also present in ceramics and photos of contemporary residents that are on display in the museum. Judging a contest based on physical characteristics is difficult enough without having to consider how well a person fits popular conceptions of the Indigenous past. That said, the pageant is designed so the winner is a resident of Salango or a surrounding community, despite the fact that it encourages participation from outside members.

I stood with the two other judges at the center of the festivities. One of the other judges was a female university student from Quito, and the other was the soundman for a German documentary filmmaker who was filming the festivities. The contestants formed a line in front of us and then walked a wide loop around us as each of their names was called. Photographers from the national and international press took photos as the crowd clapped for each contestant. Each of the girls wore an intricately designed costume that represented her cultural background. The girls from Salango and surrounding communities wore "Indigenous" costumes made of palm fronds, shells, and even maize. The eventual winner wore a crown of *Spondylus*, the de facto symbol of Salango past and present.

Following the election of la Señorita Manteña Bonita, people moved closer to the shoreline to watch the launch of the balsa. The launching of the raft is the main attraction associated with the festival, and the task requires dozens of people. The multi-ton raft is slowly pushed into the crashing surf of the Pacific Ocean. As people scramble to climb on to the raft, a rope is thrown out from the bow, where it is picked up and tied to a motorized boat. The boat slowly pulls the balsa out to sea until it clears the mooring lines of various boats in the harbor. Once clear, the balsa is released to sail on its own. The destination is Isla Salango, the most prominent physical feature of the village. The uninhabited island is approximately 2 kilometers off the coast and is believed by locals to have had cultural significance for the earliest inhabitants of the community. In a very real sense, the local landscape is used to define notions of identity and community. The festival focuses clearly on a definable space that extends from the beach to the island. Nearly all the activities associated with the festival take place in this area. By launching the balsa raft, the community reestablishes a set of natural and social referents to establish notions of locality and cultural identity. Moreover, by visiting the space between the beach and the island, participants make note of their sense of ownership and their identification with significant components of their natural environment—the same components that play a role in the everyday lives of the community, as outlined in chapter 2.

The trip to the island and back is a short journey that takes little more than one hour, depending on the prevailing winds. The triumphant return of the balsa to the beach marks the continuation of Manteño identity in its contemporary form while simultaneously confirming local relationships to space and the natural environment. At the same time, the boundaries between past and present dissolve as the barriers separating participants and onlookers are removed so all may interact and commingle on the beach and the nearby boardwalk, where music accompanies representative dances of the various invited groups.

Tilley suggests that the Día de la Raza was created to help promote the dominant ideology of mestizaje through the establishment of an "identity community" (Tilley 2005:60). The festival represents an alternative understanding by highlighting cultural heritage and Indigenous ancestry while at the same fostering and reinforcing a sense of community. Moreover, it is a performance that makes a statement about identity to guests and onlookers. This is even more the case for the manifestation of the festival that takes place in the bustling tourist town of Puerto López (see Smith 2015). The festival represents the concrete expression of collective identity while simultaneously rejecting the dominant paradigm of mestizaje. Thus, the Día de la Raza has been transformed in Salango so as not to celebrate mestizo identity but instead to celebrate Indigenous ancestry while also making claims about identity in the present.[2]

CELEBRATING THE PAST

Similar to the festival, the museum in Salango represents a space for asserting identity and contemporary connections to the past by way of the archaeological record. I returned to Salango in the fall of 2007 and was soon recruited to help organize the celebration of the museum's twentieth anniversary. The museum is one of the most prominent yet often ignored symbols of Salango's prehistory. Founded in 1987 by archaeologist Presley Norton, the museum has remained a working research center since its inception. Throughout its history it has been under the financial and managerial direction of *Fundación Presley Norton*, an international NGO (*Fundación Pro Pueblo*), and most recently the comuna Salango. The establishment of the museum as cultural patrimony of the comuna occurred in 2005 following the withdrawal of funding by Fundación Pro Pueblo that was linked in part to local land disputes between the NGO director and the local community.

The idea for the celebration of the museum's anniversary was actually a bit of an accident. Concerned members of the community met to discuss some minor grievances over the museum's management and the treatment of a French researcher who was working out of the museum at the time. Individuals at the meeting, mostly younger members of the community, began to discuss the history of the museum while noting that the twentieth anniversary was just a few weeks away. From that improbable moment, the idea to organize a communal celebration was born.

Led in large part by Diego and other engaged community members, the group organizing the anniversary celebration worked tirelessly over the following two weeks. The celebration grew quickly from what was originally conceived of as an intimate gathering of community members and beneficiaries to a guest list that included the reigning queen of Manabí province; various international guests, including numerous scholars and researchers who had contributed to the museum and the original excavations conducted by Norton; and a highland Kichwa shaman who would perform a ritual cleansing and blessing. Despite the diversity of invitees, the organizing group remained dedicated to the original intent of having a museum open house for the community. This was a significant step, considering that the museum had never had an anniversary celebration and most community residents had never set foot inside the museum. In fact, prior to 2005, the museum was a space that was largely controlled by outsiders in the form of archaeologists and the previously mentioned Fundación Pro Pueblo. While the museum was *about* the community, it was not *of* the community.

The festivities for the anniversary included the open house, a cleansing ceremony and blessing, presentations by local school groups, including a rousing

FIGURE 3.5. *Children gather outside the museum for the anniversary celebration.*

reenactment of Pizarro's encounter with the Indigenous inhabitants of the Ecuadorian coast, and speeches by local and regional officials. The entire day revolved around a single theme that was the celebration of identity, the Indigenous past, and the Indigenous present.

The open house represented a means of linking the past and the present. Although it was about the museum, it was equally about the community. Teenagers from the local high school, who had received informational lectures on archaeology and the museum, ushered in groups of community residents and explained the significance of the museum and its contents. It was an attempt to bring the community into the museum to inform residents about the prehistory of their community and also to acknowledge the museum as a community institution. At the same time, inviting community members to tour the museum symbolically reduced the distance between residents and the archaeological record.

The shamanic cleansing and blessing followed the open house and had a very different purpose. The cleansing sent an implicit message about power, authority, and Indigenous identity. Numerous attendees commented that the shaman had performed a cleansing ritual and blessing at the inauguration of Ecuadorian president Rafael Correa, and having him in Salango was not only important for community members but also represented a growing awareness of the importance of Salango. Perhaps Diego's assertion about Salango not being on the map was not so true after all.

FIGURE 3.6. *Shamanic presentation at the museum anniversary celebration*

As a well-known and respected figure of Indigenous authority, the shaman's presence at the anniversary signified the authority of the cabildo and its ability to tap into an ever-growing Ecuadorian Indigenous discourse, a discourse that was also used to help promote development activities throughout the community, as discussed in detail in forthcoming chapters. Throughout the brief blessing he said a prayer in Kichwa and spoke of recuperating local culture and valuing the past while referencing Salango as an Indigenous community with deep "*raíces ancestrales*" (ancestral roots). The speech was not detached from ongoing political tensions in Salango at the time or from an ongoing community struggle in which identity played a central role.

Following the presentation, various local and regional officials and members of the archaeological community presented their thoughts about the importance of the day and the prominence of the museum in the community. Eduardo, one of the leaders in organizing the celebration, championed Salango as "the most important place [site] on the Pacific coast" (Bauer 2014:326). Dressed in a neatly pressed shirt and Panama hat, the president of the regional chamber of tourism maintained, "we have not lost this identity." The identity to which he was referring was the "Native" identity of the

Ecuadorian coast. Comuna president Roberto Toledo continued the theme by again reiterating the ancestral roots of the community as a defining feature of contemporary identity.

Salangueños conceive of their own identity with reference to the archaeological record and its role not only in the commonplace activities associated with life in a rural village but also in the instances of ceremony and festivity. While there is a gap between the past and the present, "The past is preserved in the present, but it is imperfectly preserved, both because of entropic transformations of the structures of the past and because of loss of information" (Aberle 1987:556). Even so, residents utilize their knowledge of the past to substantiate claims about identity in the present, in a manner similar to that referenced by Friedman (1992:853) where "subjects in the present fashion the past in the practice of their social identity." The result is a conceptualization of identity that is fashioned from a "subjective antiquity" (Anderson 1983:14) in which residents "infuse representations and discourses with elements of their own making" (Radcliffe 2000:167). Such representations have implications for local politics and claims about identity (Bauer 2014). In chapter 4 I address these consequences while examining the formal emergence of an Indigenous discourse in Salango.

NOTES

1. Various museums throughout the region, including Museo Salango, establish a link between the Manteño and current residents by placing images of Manteño ceramics next to images of contemporary residents. The images highlight the Manteño nose as a marker of continuity.

2. Smith (2015) relates a similar account in her book that focuses on the nearby community of Agua Blanca.

4

The year 1990 marked a critical time in the history of Indigenous politics in Ecuador. It is perhaps best known for the national Indigenous Uprising, or levantamiento indígena, that began with the Indigenous occupation of the Catholic Cathedral of Santo Domingo in the Ecuadorian capital of Quito.[1] The cathedral was built between 1581 and 1650 and is a symbol of Spanish colonial conquest and the continued inequalities and legacy of colonialism. Beneath the cathedral plaza is a prehistoric Indigenous burial site that predates Spanish arrival in the Americas (Becker 2010; Whitten 1996). The choice of Indigenous Ecuadorians, mostly of highland Kichwa origin, to occupy the cathedral was a symbolic proclamation as much as a physical statement of resistance to hegemony and a declaration of the desire for equal citizenship.

The protest at the Cathedral of Santo Domingo was the beginning of what would become the largest Indigenous mobilization in Ecuador, a mobilization in which major roadways were occupied by tens of thousands of protestors, and highland cities—including Ambato, Latacunga, and Riobamba—were cut off. In addition, roadways connecting the coast, highlands, and Amazonian lowlands were occupied, causing an economic standstill. Throughout the country there were boycotts of markets, occupations of government buildings, and marches demonstrating resistance. The goal of the massive protest, coordinated by Ecuador's national Indigenous federation, CONAIE

Indigeneity in Uncommon Places

Representation, Plurinationalism, and the Multiple Meanings of Indigeneity

DOI: 10.5876/9781607327608.c004

(Confederation of Indigenous Nationalities of Ecuador), sought to bring attention to the country's persistent inequalities and served as a public call for change. Central to this was the questioning of the "uninational" state and the associated mestizo national identity (Cruz Rodríguez 2012). Benavides (2011:257) notes that the protests marked the beginning of a "post-patriarchal phase" in Ecuador in which Ecuadorian Indians took it upon themselves to push for change as opposed to relying on outside support, including the state, the Catholic Church, and other institutions.

Just as the Cathedral of Santo Domingo held deep symbolic significance, so did the decision to occupy roads. To control roads is to constrain commerce and exert influence over interactions. Symbolically, the control of roads represents power over access to belonging, and to control a road is to have a voice and a means of negotiation. Fourteen years after the levantamiento indígena, the people of Salango would stage their own protest and stake claim to their own road.

FRAMING RESISTANCE: HISTORICAL
ANTECEDENTS AND MESTIZAJE

Ethnic-based movements have been a prominent feature of the Ecuadorian ethno-political landscape for decades, and the 1990 levantamiento indígena is just one example. Mobilizations focusing on land reform date back to the 1940s. While the mobilizations vary in their manifestations, they have served to bring about awareness of hegemony and, as Warren (1998:5) asserts, to "expose the contradictions inherent in political systems that embrace democratic egalitarianism yet, by promulgating monoethnic, monocultural, and monolingual images of a modern nation, epistemically exclude major sectors of their populations." Selverston-Scher (2001) notes that Indigenous residents of Ecuador are not fully afforded citizenship rights. Evidence of this is the fact that they received the right to vote as recently as 1979. Ecuador's Indigenous movements and mobilizations aim to bring about change while calling attention to inequalities and imbalances present in the country. The mobilizations of Indigenous peoples in Ecuador are emblematic of a global shift in recognition of colonialism's legacy and the struggle for power and equal rights by individuals and groups who have been the victims of ethnic marginalization.

Mestizaje is at the core of the previously mentioned process of ethnic marginalization, and early champions of mestizaje—including Simón Bolívar, José Martí, and José Vasconcelos—viewed mestizaje as an organizing principle that would overcome diversity and create the cultural and ethnic cohesion needed to achieve the progress of the nation-state. The writings of Vasconcelos typified the implicit and sometimes explicit racism inherent within the ideology of mestizaje.

It is necessary to problematize the notion of race as it pertains to Latin America to understand the implications of Vasconcelos's work. While the term *race* is often used to refer to phenotypic markers such as skin tone, facial structure, and hair color and texture, contemporary anthropologists recognize that race has very little biological significance. Instead, race is a culturally constructed category that uses phenotypic characteristics as a means of creating social distance and differential access to power. Vasconcelos uses the term *race* not in a strictly phenotypical sense but with reference to cultural markers perceived as defining difference. For Vasconcelos and most scholars of mestizaje, the process of mestizaje and the creation of mestizo identities reflect the coming together of various phenotypic and cultural features in the form of a homogenized identity. Thus, mestizaje occurs not so much through biological mixing as through acculturation and assimilation. However, from a historical perspective, it is significant that biological mixing was a prominent component of Latin American contact, conquest, and colonization (Esteva-Fabregat 1994; Wade 1997). In my own experiences in Salango, I have found that many residents do recognize phenotype as a foundational component of identity. This is manifest as people refer to themselves as *mezclados* (mixed) or point to things such as having *rasgos indígenas* (Indigenous racial features).

Writing on indigeneity in Mexico, Borah asserts that "by the end of the eighteenth century, racial mixture had proceeded so far that there were few pure bloods left in the country" and concludes that "with few exceptions, then, it seems that Indians have disappeared in Mexico as separate ethnic groups" (Borah 1954:341–42). Borah's statements lend power to the process of mestizaje as a mechanism of homogenization. However, much like Vasconcelos, Borah struggles to disentangle the meanings of race and ethnicity. More recent work by Weismantel (2000) illustrates similar complexities with regard to "race rape" and the meanings of whiteness as contrasted with indigeneity in the Peruvian Andes. In this, the violent act of physical rape dehumanizes Indigenous women while also violating Indigenous culture and asserting white superiority, the product of which is the mestizo. While mestizaje appears to promote synthesis and cohesion, it does so at the cost of Indigenous ethnic components. European components, those with higher cultural value, are preferred over Indigenous elements as a contribution to national identity; and difference, in this case indigeneity, becomes a barrier to progress and attaining a cohesive national identity. However, central to this discussion is the notion that identities are context-dependent; how indigeneity is defined, as well as who is defined as Indigenous, varies dependent on perspective and position (Martínez Novo 2006).

The issue of power is central to any discussion of mestizaje, and boundaries are demarcated between Indigenous and non-Indigenous members of society in a manner compatible with Barth's (1998) classic work on ethnicity and boundary making.[2] A central tenant of Barth's analysis is that an ethnic group is defined not so much by "the cultural stuff that it encloses" but by the social and cultural boundaries that define the group in contrast to other groups (Barth 1998:15). While such boundaries are often territorial, they are also marked by differences in behavior. And in some cases, perceived differences are as important as actual differences in culture or behavior. A brief example will illustrate this point.

When returning to Ecuador in the spring of 2006, I met a young man named Pablo on my flight from Miami to Quito. It was one of the rare occasions when I stopped in Quito before continuing on to Guayaquil. We began talking as we waited for takeoff. Pablo, who was from Quito, asked my reason for going to Ecuador and where I was going. I explained that I was going to Guayaquil and then on to Manabí to continue my dissertation fieldwork. He was surprised that Manabí was my destination and asked what I was interested in studying. In the brief conversation that followed, I provided an abridged version of my focus on identity and development, and I mentioned "*la politica de los grupos Indígenas*" (Indigenous politics). Pablo was surprised and immediately responded that I should be working in *la sierra* (the highlands) and not *la costa* (the coast). For Pablo, Indigenous groups did not exist on the coast. While this reflects boundaries in a geographical sense, it does not get to the heart of the ideas presented by Barth (1998). As our discussion continued into the flight, I asked Pablo about someone who is born and raised Indigenous and ultimately acculturates and achieves a "mestizo" cultural identity. Pablo asserted, "*Igual son Indios*" (They are still Indians). He did not make the statement with any notable disrespect in his voice. To the contrary, his delivery was quite matter-of-fact. He went on to provide an example of a young woman with whom he studied at the university. He told me that she lives in Quito and has a good job, and even though she might continue to move up in her job, she is still regarded as "*una India*" (an Indian). What struck me in the conversation was that Pablo, a self-identifying mestizo, did not refer to his acquaintance in a disparaging manner but simply used the ethnic marker of Indio to designate difference. This is quite different from frequent uses of the word "Indio" in a more derogatory manner. However, in all cases its use signifies difference;

within the ethno-racial hierarchy that is present in Ecuador, to be Indio is to be of less value than mestizo. Moreover, while such boundaries may be arbitrarily drawn and differences are frequently essentialized for instrumental and political purposes, ethnic boundaries are linked to embedded social and cultural meanings that highlight actual or perceived differences in the process of boundary making. These cultural meanings form the cornerstone of mestizaje in both its past and contemporary forms. A core component of this is referenced by Martínez Novo (2006) in her writings on Indigenous identities in northern Mexico. She suggests that culture and interpretations of culture serve as justifications for exclusion of access to socioeconomic resources while also calling attention to the hierarchical nature of ethnic identities and meanings associated with mestizaje. The underlying concept in the work of both Barth (1998) and Martínez Novo (2006) is difference. However, it is not enough to merely recognize difference as fundamental to understanding mestizaje. It is imperative to ask questions about when and how differences are expressed and the reasons for such expressions of difference.

A particularly appropriate way to understand mestizaje is to reference what Stutzman (1981:45) calls "an all-inclusive ideology of exclusion." As a classificatory system, mestizaje masks differences within groups while exaggerating differences between groups. Thus, for many Ecuadorians all Indians are the same, and this sameness often carries negative connotations. One August evening I sat conversing with friends and acquaintances along the malecón. As we talked about the day's events, the conversation shifted to a discussion about ethnic identity. While this might seem out of the ordinary, it was appropriate for the moment. "We are not Indios. Other communities are, but not us. Ugly Indios . . . they are ugly, you know that," proclaimed Oscar with anger. When I heard the comment, I was both taken aback and curious. I was surprised by the ease with which the comment was made, and I was intrigued because that was the very day representatives from CONAIE had arrived in Salango to meet with community leaders about Indigenous rights. Realizing this paradox, the commentary about the ugliness of "Indians" versus the meeting about Indigenous rights, I took the opportunity to dig deeper. During the conversation I was continually reminded of the ugliness of Indians as Oscar spoke about vendors from the highlands who frequent the village going door to door selling clothing, CDs and DVDs, and fresh produce. What I came away with from that exchange is that Oscar, not unlike Clara, attempted to position himself within the framework of mestizaje by asserting difference and establishing boundaries between his community and other communities throughout the region.

As mentioned earlier, contemporary ethnic politics in Ecuador is a legacy of colonialism. The historical foundation of this legacy merits further examination. In the past, Ecuador's diverse Indigenous groups were treated in much the same way Oscar referred to Indios—as the other, lumped together for the sake of convenience for those in power. The various Indigenous groups inhabiting Ecuador's highland, coastal, and Amazonian regions—who spoke different languages, carried out different cultural practices, and were from diverse environmental and geographic environments—were transformed into "Indians" under Spanish rule. This designation of difference buttressed a developing ethno-racial hierarchy, and legal distinctions were made on this basis. As in much of Latin America, Spanish settlement in Ecuador occurred rapidly, and the Spanish Crown restructured Indigenous social organization in the aftermath of conquest. One result of this was the legal separation of Indigenous populations from whites and mestizos by way of the constitution of *La República de los Indios* (the Indian Republic). Indigenous populations were given a separate set of laws and rights in a process that formalized difference. This extended to the *encomienda* system in Ecuador, predicated on allocating land to individuals in service to the Crown. These individuals controlled not only land but also production and labor. Indians were required to pay tribute to the *encomendero* for his protection and allowance of the use of land for production. This tribute system, known as "Indian Tribute," was also associated with *reducciones:*[3] "The natives were to be collected from their hills and resettled in conveniently accessible valleys, in Spanish-style villages . . . They offered much resistance to this plan which facilitated the collection of taxes, strengthened Church control of the population, removed the native groups from their sacred shrines and burying grounds, and frequently brought together people of diverse ethnic affiliations" (Murra 1963:814).

While encomiendas and reducciones increased Spanish control over Indigenous populations, the policies and practices also reinforced the dissimilarities between whites and Indians through formal, structural means. This extended past Ecuadorian independence in 1822 and well beyond the abolishment of the tribute system in 1857. Whereas the end of tribute theoretically extended regular citizenship to Indians, the politics of difference persisted through the continuation of the hacienda system in a manner Pallares (2002:11) describes as "a closed, corporate system in which haciendas ensured the social control of Indians by providing needed goods and services that increased their debts and by preventing them from seeking work in villages and cities." In effect, the Indigenous-white relations established during the colonial period continued well into the twentieth century through the maintenance of the hacienda system and debt peonage. It was not until 1964 that land reform brought a formal end to the hacienda system and the labor relations that had typified Indigenous-white relations since the colonial period.

In post-reform Ecuador (post-1964), to be Indigenous is still to be stigmatized, to be an outsider; for far too long, Ecuador's Indigenous peoples have been viewed as obstacles to be overcome. Agricultural reform in the 1960s marked a shift from the "Indian problem" being conceptualized as a local concern to a national concern (Lucero 2003:40). Recent discussions pertaining to natural resource extraction in Indigenous territories of Ecuador's Amazon illustrate this point. In 2013 Ecuadorian archbishop emeritus José Mario Ruiz Navas presented a critique of policies that justify oil exploration on Indigenous lands located within the boundaries of Ecuador's Yasuní Reserve. The archbishop questioned the dismissal of Indigenous Ecuadorians as "solo indios" (just Indians) as he commented on the case of territorial rights and the development of Ecuador's Amazon (Ruiz Navas 2013). The case relates to the shifting political position of the administration of former president Rafael Correa, who received strong Indigenous support when he ran for office in 2006. This support was based largely on Correa's stance against neo-liberalism and extractivism in Indigenous territories. Correa's position changed, and extractive resource exploitation in the Yasuní Reserve was supported by his administration prior to leaving office in 2017 (Abbot 2013).

The marginalization of Indigenous populations and the politics of difference result in a situation in which the acceptance of mestizaje and corresponding acculturation and assimilation become an avenue for inclusion. Based on work in Bolivia, Canessa (2006:245) notes that "the mestizo was part of the national project of creating an urban, Spanish-speaking middle class . . . and consequently, the indian was erased in favor of a mestizo identity." Reck (1986) provides a notable account of this as he traces the challenges faced by a young Mexican man of Indigenous ancestry who struggles with his own identity and acceptance into the dominant mestizo society. What becomes clear from these and similar accounts, such as the noted text *Los Ríos Profundos* by Peruvian author José María Arguedas, is that European-ness holds a more esteemed value than Indigenousness in the making of national identities. Arguedas writes, "He was a tall man who dressed like a mestizo, wearing a necktie and leather leggings . . . He spoke Spanish, but when he became annoyed he *lost control* of himself and insulted his son in Quechua" (Arguedas 2002:52, emphasis added). Here, to be Indigenous is to lack control in the same way unruly mestizo children are often rebuked by elders for acting like "indios." While official discourses of mestizaje in Ecuador do not directly reference Indigenous

Ecuadorians in the manner presented by Arguedas, what is clear in examining the historical treatment of Indigenous Ecuadorians is that they are positioned on the margins of Ecuadorian national identity, as is the case with the comments made by Rodríguez Lara and the case of Clara I presented in chapter 1.

Moreover, expressions of ethnicity are "countercultural because ethnicity entails nonconformity . . . and dissent" (Stutzman 1981:76). The result is a cultural context in which non-mestizos are expected to assimilate into the dominant mestizo culture (León 1994). As Weismantel (2003:327) notes, expressions of indigeneity, such as the use of traditional Indigenous dress in Ecuador, instill "fearful visions of a nation dragged backward by its non-white citizens, who by stubbornly refusing to adopt national culture, subvert the desires of a nation anxious to achieve and consolidate modernity." Returning to 1990, the levantamiento indígena was not heralded as a moment of "Indigenous uprising" by all. Mainstream news outlets portrayed the events as the *alzamiento indígena* (Indigenous revolt). The difference in wording is significant. As opposed to the levantamiento, or "rising up," of Indigenous Ecuadorians, the term *alzamiento* carries a connotation of revolt or insurgency and is associated with "indians out of control or blacks out of control . . . getting out of place, lacking consciousness, and acting in an unruly manner" (Whitten and Whitten 2011:76). Of note is that there is no equivalent usage of the term *alzamiento* in Spanish as applied to whites (Whitten and Whitten 2011). The perpetual marginalization of Indigenous people as second-class citizens has only recently been met by significant challenges that call into question the very nature of mestizaje and its meanings in contemporary Latin America.

INDIGENOUS MOVEMENTS AND POLITICS IN ECUADOR

Indigenous movements in Ecuador represent a response to centuries of pervasive difference established firmly on the ideological foundations put forth by mestizaje. The growth of Ecuador's pan-ethnic movement can be traced to a formative period prior to the 1960s in which ethnic and class politics overlapped (Becker 1997, 1999, 2008; Pallares 2002; Selverston-Scher 2001; Yashar 2005). During the 1960s and 1970s, Indigenous politics was geographically centered in the highlands, and land was a central feature of Indigenous political interests. The Andean Indigenous organization known as *Ecuador Runacunapac Richarimui* (ECUARUNARI) was formed in 1973 in Tepeyac, Chimborazo (the name means "the Ecuadorian Indian Awakens") (Pallares 2002). With support from liberation theologians associated with the Catholic Church, ECUARUNARI sought to unite Andean Indigenous populations of all backgrounds in a common struggle for land and citizenship rights. Unlike previous organizations throughout the Ecuadorian highlands, ECUARUNARI focused specifically on Indigenous struggles and identity.

Just as ECUARUNARI formed an umbrella under which various local and regional Indigenous organizations of the highlands could coordinate, *CONFENAIE* (Confederación de Nacionalidades Indígenas de la Amazonia del Ecuador) was formed in 1980 in an effort to coordinate Amazonian groups and defend Indigenous cultures and territory (Yashar 2005). In a manner similar to ECUARUNARI, the development of CONFENAIE was a direct response to Ecuadorian land reform. By the 1980s both CONFENAIE and ECUARUNARI sought inclusion in the Ecuadorian state through equal access to citizenship rights and Indigenous autonomy.[4] The formation of regional Indigenous organizations in the highlands and the Amazon ultimately led to the growth of Ecuador's national Indigenous organization CONAIE. CONAIE was established in 1986 after years of strategic planning by the leaders of ECUARUNARI and CONFENAIE.

CONAIE is a powerful voice for the struggles of Indigenous peoples in Ecuador, and its success is heavily dependent on the establishment of a "national Indigenous identity." This identity was something that had not existed previously, since Ecuador's Indigenous populations vary dramatically in their linguistic and cultural characteristics. CONFENAIE alone represented eight Indigenous nationalities in 1992: the Shuar, Kichwa, Achuar, Shiwiar, Siona, Secoya, Cofán, and Huaorani (Sawyer 2004). To establish the aforementioned "national Indigenous identity," CONAIE's leaders focused not on the vast differences that exist between participating Indigenous nationalities but instead on the similar struggle shared by all Indigenous groups in Ecuador. This struggle for state recognition of Indigenous rights has been broadly framed to allow for a high degree of fluidity and flexibility.

Ultimately, CONAIE attempts to create unity where discontinuity and difference dominate the cultural landscape and essentialization functions to form a cohesive movement. Warren and Jackson (2002:8) use the term *essentialism* to refer to "discourses of enduring commonalities—common ethnic roots and historical pasts, cultural essences, and experiences that are seen as naturally binding people together." Despite the cultural disparities that exist between the various Indigenous nationalities that form CONAIE, all groups share similar histories of oppression, subordination, and domination. Thus, history and power, or, more accurately, shared histories and shared relations to power, are the ties that unite the various Indigenous nationalities represented by CONAIE.[5]

Discussions of Indigenous politics and identities in Ecuador rarely mention the Ecuadorian coast. At the beginning of my research in 2002, there was little reason to question this, and there was little mention of indigeneity or Indigenous politics in Salango. The reasons for the lack of reference are numerous. A rather simplistic explanation is that the Ecuadorian coast does not have a substantial Indigenous population; therefore, Indigenous politics has been of little consequence on the coast. In fact, many of my consultants were quick to point out that they are mezclados (mixed) and that Indigenous people are from la sierra and el oriente (the Amazon). Demographic data support this contention inasmuch as a regional perspective suggests that less than 2 percent of the total population of the Ecuadorian coastal provinces of El Oro, Esmeraldas, Guayas, Los Ríos, and Manabí is Indigenous (Van Cott 2005).[6] However, a demographic explanation is problematic, not only because it attempts to quantify culturally recognized conceptions of identity that are heavily dependent on frames of interaction but also because it neglects to take into account the history of the region and how that history has shaped localized understandings of identity. As my work shows, groups that trace their ancestry to past Indigenous populations have not historically been considered Indigenous; nor have they necessarily demonstrated a self-asserted Indigenous identity.

As related previously, the Ecuadorian coast, particularly Manabí province, has been popularly classified as mestizo or in some instances "montubio," even if locals do not self-identify with either of these labels.[7] The term montubio is complex but tends to be associated geographically with Guayas, Manabí, and Santa Elena provinces and references peasant farmers of the region who are of mixed descent. Moreover, the term generally carries negative connotations such as ignorant, backward, and uncultured (see Bauer 2012; Roitman 2008, 2009; Whitten 1965 for more detail).

Until recently, the Indigenous heritage of coastal Manabí's communities has too often been relegated to the local museums, such as Museo Salango, and the occasional festival celebrating Indigenous heritage, such as the balsa festival outlined in chapter 3. However, the 1990s ushered in a period of heightened ethnic awareness on the coast, as throughout much of the country. Preceded by Indigenous organizing in the highlands and the Amazon, coastal populations began to reframe their collective identity. A brief outline of that history will provide context for the forthcoming discussion in this and the following chapters.

Beginning in the late 1980s, peasants of Indigenous descent residing throughout the coastal provinces of Guayas and Manabí, who had long been regarded as ethnically mestizo or montubio, organized to reassert their Indigenous heritage and stake claim to their identity. Álvarez (1999) argues that the growth of Indigenous politics along the south coast of Ecuador can be attributed to a shift in ethnic consciousness in which coastal peasants who were recognized as mestizo or montubio pushed for acknowledgment of collective rights by adopting a discourse of Indigeneity and ancestrality.

Following this initial step in 1988, residents of Guayas and Manabí provinces collectively organized to form *El Movimiento Indígena de los Pueblos Manta Wankavilkas y Punaés* (MIPMAWPU) in 2000, with the main objective being to gain recognition for the Indigenous groups of the Ecuadorian coast (Bazurco Osorio 2006). According to official statistics from the CODENPE (*Consejo de Desarrollo de las Nacionalidades y Pueblos del Ecuador*) website, approximately 168,000 individuals in 318 communities form the Pueblo Manta-Wankavilkas.

THE ROAD TO CHANGE

E15 is the winding coastal highway that leads north from the Santa Elena peninsula, through the rugged hills of southern Manabí and to the north beyond Salango. The significance of E15 for Salango and neighboring communities is that it is the only thoroughfare that links Salango to any major destination in Ecuador. The closest southern access or departure point is approximately 100 km south of Salango, and the closest northern access or departure point is nearly 50 km to the north. Salango is literally a village with one road in and one road out—the same road leading in different directions.

Prior to the 1970s, much of E15 was little more than a dirt road that was only occasionally traveled by vehicles. Community elders can recount a childhood in which a 6 km trip to the nearest market town required a difficult daylong journey by donkey over the steep hills that separate Salango from its nearest neighbor to the north. As recently as the early 2000s, much of the road was unpaved, and during the rainy season the trip to the south was precarious.

The development of E15 into a two-lane road brought significant changes to Salango. Improvements allowed for better methods of transportation and increased access to consumer goods from the port cities of Guayaquil and Manta. At the same time, the local fishing economy was bolstered by the availability of new technologies and access to markets. By the early 1980s it was routine for fish to be loaded into trucks in the early morning hours and shipped directly to the urban centers of Guayaquil, Manta, Salinas, and Libertad.

Consultants of mine reflected on these changes in a variety of ways. Most notably, village elders lamented the fact that the activities of their youth, hiking into the nearby *montaña* to work the fields and harvest coffee, had been replaced almost entirely by a focus on the ocean and the booming fishing industry. Younger residents of the village recall a childhood in which the dense vegetation of the montaña seemingly reached the sand of the beach with little interruption. This is in stark contrast with the village today, where the vegetation reaches only as far as the highway and does not extend the kilometer or so toward the beach.

The integration of Salango into broader Ecuadorian society, resultant from the advances of E15, can be linked to changes far more profound than the economic ones I have mentioned thus far. The roadway opened Salango to archaeologists both national and foreign, as excavations began at the site where a large multinational fishmeal factory now resides on the south end of the beach. Those excavations gave way to the archaeological presence outlined in chapter 3 and would serve as the groundwork for forthcoming claims about identity, communal politics, and development.

It was the summer of 2004, and tensions in Salango had been building for years. Casual conversations frequently turned to the local political situation and questions about the sale of communal land a few years earlier. Internally, the struggle was between the comuna and those who opposed its action to sell communal land in 1999. This same sale pitted community members not only against one another but also against a powerful outsider who had been making inroads into the comuna for a number of years. Referred to locally as el gringo or *El Suizo*, his charitable foundation, Fundación Pro Pueblo, provided funding for the local museum and at one time ran a number of small development projects in and around Salango. His influence was significant. My experiences with him were limited to a single conversation and frequent sightings of him driving through the town's dirt streets in a high-end SUV. Locals frequently speculated about him and his goings on, and rumors ran rampant. One memorable rumor is that famous Colombian singer Shakira visited him and his family on their private beach just south of the village. Residents spoke frequently about what they perceived to be his intentions for a large plot of land (34 hectares) he purchased from the comuna in 1999.

At the same time residents were entrenched in discussions of the local political situation, they were also paying keen attention to a local construction project. The malecón was the only paved road at the time, and there was a plan to widen and pave the main road coming into town from E15. The road in question leads past the museum and ends on the beach. A turn to the left before hitting the beach leads one onto the malecón. The only foreseeable problem with the construction was that it would require demolishing an exterior wall of the museum to widen the road. Adding to the problem was the fact that the exterior wall was part of numerous small cabins that housed researchers and students when they visited the museum for extended periods of time.

Anxiety built in the days leading up to the construction, and speculation abounded. What would happen if the construction went as planned and the wall was demolished? Would El Suizo and his foundation still support the museum? If they pulled their support for the museum, how would it survive? The general sentiment was that going through with construction and the demolition of the wall would anger El Suizo and perhaps drive him away from the museum and the community. Most locals avoided him and even feared him. While many recognized that he did contribute to the community when he first arrived, he was rumored to be vengeful and full of hate when things did not go his way. The project proceeded, and funding was pulled from the museum. Community members, led by Roberto Toledo, pushed for control of the museum, with the goal of making it a community museum and rightfully placing Salango's cultural patrimony in the hands of its residents, as opposed to the hands of a wealthy gringo. The inner workings of the museum transfer played out rather quietly, and what appeared to be of great significance throughout town was the fact that El Suizo's ties to Salango had been significantly reduced.

Stress continued in the weeks following the transfer, and local community leaders organized to bring attention to the conflict involving communal land sold illegally, according to Toledo and his supporters. On July 16, 2004, residents gathered at the south end of the village to protest the sale of the land and El Suizo's presence in the community. Highway E15 was the location of the resistance. The *carretera* (highway) was blocked with tires, large oil drums filled with soil, rocks, and other types of debris that would prevent the passage of vehicles into the village from the south. The action, known throughout Ecuador as a *paro* (strike or protest), replicated, albeit on a far reduced scale, the types of paros associated with the 1990 levantamiento indígena and subsequent protests in 1992 and 2001. The dispute over the sale of communal land was the center point of contestation, and village leaders presented the government with a list of demands. Headlining the list was the demand that the comuna Salango receive official government recognition as an Indigenous community.

Claims to land emphasized a historical attachment to place and stressed the archaeological record as support in much the same way Selverston-Scher (2001:82) argues that land is "an integral part of cultural reproduction" and therefore maintains a prominent place in the life of most Indigenous movements. For Salangueños who opposed the sale of communal land, one of the fundamental problems was that the land was relegated to commodity status. It was no longer part of the communal realm of economic interaction. By allowing the land to be sold, the Ecuadorian government was negating Salangueños' claims regarding ancestral territory. While claims to territory have clear political implications, they are also significant for establishing a sense of identity and belonging.

The Ministry of Agriculture, to which the community of Salango was administratively dependent at the time of the sale, responded to the residents' claims by asserting that the sale was legal because the residents of Salango were classified as montubio or mestizo as opposed to Indigenous. The argument made by the Ecuadorian state used ethnicity as a legitimizing factor in the sale of the land by suggesting that as montubios, the people of Salango were not afforded the same rights to communal land as Ecuador's Indigenous residents, even though the 1937 Ley de Comunas and subsequent reform laws of 1964 and 1973 were not aimed solely at Indigenous populations (Becker 1999). Thus, the issue of land tenure and the corresponding question of appropriate development became entangled in questions of ethnicity and citizenship rights (Bauer 2010a).

Whereas the Ecuadorian government recognized the inhabitants of Salango as montubio or mestizo, community leaders in Salango argued for formal recognition of indigeneity based on their historical connection to the region's Indigenous past. By focusing on indigeneity and the ancestral ties presented in chapter 3, residents established a connection to an Indigenous discourse that had gained prominence throughout Ecuador. Moreover, community leaders who opposed the sale of the land and were acutely aware of the influence of Indigenous politics in Ecuador began to frame their own struggle as an ethnic struggle. This ability to link up ideologically proved a powerful means of gaining national attention.

Framing identity in this way is not unique. Gordon and Hale (2003) relate a similar account about land claims on the Nicaraguan coast, where Indigenous and Creole peoples made claims to land by referencing their historical presence in the region and the political institutions that existed prior to the formation of the Nicaraguan state. In a manner similar to that in Salango, Nicaraguan protagonists framed their collective identity to make claims about land rights against the state. Hooker (2005) provides similar evidence in relating how territorial claims couched in terms of ethnicity as opposed to race or class have led to successful negotiation with the state by Afro-Nicaraguan communities. These communities have gained rights only when they "have been able to claim an autochthonous or 'indigenous-like' position" that emphasizes a distinct cultural group identity (Hooker 2005:304). Brondo (2010) and Latorre (2013) present analogous cases from Honduras and Ecuador, respectively. In all cases, dominant notions of identity that are imposed and reinforced by the state and that ultimately deny citizenship rights to specific groups based on identity are subject to reinterpretations (Bauer 2012).

The process of reframing identity, often as Indigenous or ancestral and frequently associated with claims to territory, is an important mechanism for negotiating with the state. In the summer of 2003, individuals who opposed the sale of the land and the anticipated development of the region formed a new cabildo, with Roberto Toledo leading the charge. This was the reason for the signatures provided by Mario and others. At the time of its creation, the Ecuadorian government did not officially recognize the new cabildo. However, the newly organized group functioned as a first step toward disputing the sale of Salango's communal land and the threat of impending development. By forming alliances with officials from CONAIE, Toledo and his supporters tapped into the strong Indigenous discourse that is present in Ecuador.

On July 12, 2004, talk of the planned paro spread throughout the normally quiet village. My daily interactions with locals often involved discussions about the upcoming protest, and at times I struggled to gain a clear understanding of exactly what was going on. Even though my interests were in other topics, including tourism development, it was hard to avoid the ongoing political tensions. This was the precarious position of a gringo anthropologist. I was accepted into the community and provided with insight, but at the time I was not fully aware of the complex set of circumstances that led to the conflict. In the early morning hours of July 16, the proposed paro came to fruition. Members of the comuna and objectors to the land sale blockaded the highway, causing all traffic moving along E15 to come to a standstill. News of the political unrest spread quickly through town. Men sat playing cards at their usual locations, either on front porches or at many of the small tiendas located throughout the town. Women stood conversing on the front stoops of homes or washing laundry on the patios. In this apparent air of normalcy, all ears were tuned to the local radio station, which broadcast coverage of the political mobilization. Interviews with leaders of the protest, including Toledo, flooded the airwaves.

Despite the continual radio coverage of the protest, widespread recognition of the unrest did not come quickly. Manuel and I spoke about the situation, and he offered to accompany me to the protest site. We walked across the village under a gray sky and light rain. Upon our arrival, we saw people huddled underneath a makeshift canopy to avoid the persistent rain. Men, women, and children were present; some families brought mattresses with the intent of settling in for the long haul. The tone was much more serious than it had been the previous day. The press had not yet arrived, and many of the protestors demonstrated clear discontent with the attention paid to them by the national government.

Two long rainy days after the protest began, a response came from Guayaquil. At approximately 6:00 a.m. on the morning of July 18, dozens of members of the national police force arrived in Salango. The once peaceful protest turned violent when the police attempted to disperse the crowd of protestors using tear gas. The national recognition the protestors desired soon followed.

After the rapid dispersal of the protestors, they reconvened in the early afternoon and marched through the streets of Salango, led by Toledo and a small contingency of young men carrying sticks and machetes. Chants of "Viva Salango" (long live Salango) and "Viva el paro" (long live the strike) shattered the silence of the village. They marched the 6 km to Puerto López and pled their case at the *municipio* (city hall). Because of their discontent with the way the national police handled the protest, the protestors demanded the resignation of the mayor of Puerto López and went so far as to call for the resignation of the provincial governor of Manabí. What was initially a local conflict between a community and a powerful outsider quickly erupted into a conflict in which people were fighting to reclaim their rights as Ecuadorian citizens—rights including access to communal lands, government recognition of Indigenous identity, and the right to protest peacefully.

The community settled back into a sense of normalcy in the following days as the number of protestors decreased and the road was opened to traffic. The pattern of fishing and daily life resumed as people went about their normal business. The protest continued, but it was not central to the goings on in the community. Sporadic radio coverage addressed the protest and people still talked about it, but it did not have the same weight it had carried in previous days. That would soon change. On July 22, six days after the paro began, the bishop of Manabí arrived in Salango. Word of his arrival spread quickly, and residents made their way to the protest site. I attended as well but stood back from the crowd so as not to insert myself into the situation. Two national police officers monitored the situation, their uniforms freshly pressed and their black patent-leather shoes providing a heavy shine that contrasted with the dense mud on which they walked. Holding his machete, don Léon, one of the most resolute supporters of the uprising, spoke intently about the situation: "We will stay here indefinitely. We are fighting for what is right. We are fighting for our community."

The bishop, a man short in stature with white hair, glasses, and light skin, spoke slowly and distinctly. He assured the protestors that even though he was not a government official, he was there to find a resolution to the conflict and to help. The conversation between the bishop and the protestors continued for over an hour. The protestors presented the bishop with their list of demands. The lengthy list included such items as gaining access to three of the community's beaches that had been closed to the public when the communal land was sold; a request for an administrative shift from the Ministry of Agriculture to the Ministry of Social Welfare; recognition as the legal cabildo of Salango, including access to the casa comunal (village hall); and designation as an Indigenous village to be classified as Pueblo Manta-Wankavilka (alternate spelling Manta-Huancavilca).[8] The decision to frame their struggle as an ethnic struggle was obviously well informed. By staking claim to the Manta-Wankavilka identity, the people of Salango were effectively able to form a direct link with the growing coastal Indigenous movement.

A few days later the national newspaper *El Universo* ran an op-ed column written by the bishop that outlined the case of Salango. Shortly after the piece ran, the "new" cabildo of Salango gained government recognition as the official cabildo. Under the watchful eye of national police, the cabildo, led by Roberto Toledo, took control of the casa communal on July 29, 2004.

The local response to the sale of communal land and the threat of outside development was successful for multiple reasons. Perhaps the most noteworthy factor was the ability of the comuna to tap into a powerful discourse that has taken center stage throughout much of Ecuador. In recognizing the ambiguous nature of ethnicity in Ecuador and subsequently framing its struggle as an Indigenous one, the comuna gained the attention of the regional government of Manabí and the national government of Ecuador. The politicalization of ethnicity set the stage for the people of Salango, who are not traditionally considered Indigenous by the state, to use their claims of ethnic identity to redefine their relationship with the Ecuadorian state while making claims about land and development.

Since 2004, the comuna Salango has continued to negotiate with the state in an attempt to strengthen its position as an Indigenous community and to secure access to ancestral lands. In 2006 the comuna joined three other comunas in the region to form *Pueblo Manta*. The self-designation "Manta" helps the member comunas, all of which are under the jurisdiction of the cantón Puerto López, to assert their own unique identity and their historical relationship to each other while at the same time distinguishing themselves from the member communities of the Pueblo Manta-Wankavilka (see Smith 2015 for a related study). The emergence of the Manta identity is a process of ethnogenesis, which is "intrinsically dynamic and rooted in a people's sense of historical consciousness" and represents "a synthesis of a people's cultural and political struggles to exist as well as their historical consciousness of these struggles" (Hill 1996:1–2). Thus, the political pressure for recognition as an Indigenous community reflects the historical set of relations Salangueños have had with outsiders, both foreign and national. Within Ecuador, Salango's Indigenous ancestry has not been recognized despite a strong outsider emphasis, in the form of archaeological findings, on the Indigenous history and prehistory of the community, referenced in chapter 3.

The establishment of the Manta identity represents a case of both constructivism and instrumentalism while also reflecting the claims to primordialism. The transition from Pueblo Manta-Wankavilka to Pueblo Manta was a strategic move by community leaders and residents. Corresponding to Sandstrom's (2008) writing on ethnogenesis and ethnicity, we see how conflict and contestation gave rise to the assertion of ethnicity as "a creative response on the part of the members of one group to domination or competition with members of another group . . . [a] conscious process of differentiation" that allows members to "construct an alternate social world in which they can succeed and prosper" (Sandstrom 2008:157). The perspective provided by Sandstrom reflects the dominant anthropological understanding of ethnic identity as constructed, negotiated, and prone to change. These same qualities are reflected in the work of Stephen (1996), who focuses on ethnic identity among the Mixtec and Zapotec of Oaxaca, Mexico. Stephen emphasizes the political dimensions and fluidity of ethnic identities. Of particular relevance for the current case is Stephen's (1996:18) assertion that while ethnicity is "improvisational, fluid, and ever-changing," it has very real connections to "political and economic power relations." The leaders of the Salango movement were wise to adopt the Manta-Wankavilka identity and then transition to the more culturally specific Manta identity. By attaching themselves first to the already established Manta-Wankavilka movement, community leaders increased their chances for success. The transition from Manta-Wankavilka to Manta was also strategic. MIPMAWPU is a large organization that is dominated by populations from Guayas province. By forming Pueblo Manta, the comuna Salango and the other three participating comunas ensured that they would not be overshadowed by the other member communities of MIPMAWPU.

A press bulletin written by former CONAIE president Luis Macas in 2007 brings to light numerous elements of the Manta struggle, including the connection between Pueblo Manta and CONAIE and the notable shift in language. The bulletin outlines the history of the conflictive relationship of the comuna Salango and the wealthy businessman El Suizo and highlights the struggle not as a class struggle but an ethnic conflict: "CONAIE rejects the intervention of Patrick Bredthauer [El Suizo] and supports the (comunidad) community of Salango so that their rights to a peaceful life and community development in accordance with their way of life continues and CONAIE calls for a government guarantee that the ancestral community (comunidad) of Salango will be the exclusive responsibility of CODENPE" (Macas 2007).[9]

A close reading of the language produced by Macas indicates a not-so-subtle transition. The statement marks an explicit shift from the use of the Spanish word *comuna* to the use of the Spanish word *comunidad* when referring to Salango, the significance of which is worth elaborating on. In Ecuador, the terms *comunidad* and *pueblo* carry connotations of a specific identity and serve to demarcate ethnic difference. The term *comuna* does not. Further, identifying as a comuna does not carry the same political weight as identifying as a pueblo or comunidad. Identification as a pueblo or comunidad allows for the ability to leverage political capital by establishing links to any number of Indigenous institutions, including, but not limited to, CONAIE. In addition, multiple villages, hamlets, and towns that may not be part of the same comuna establish political links through the use of the terms *pueblo, nacionalidad* (nationality), or *comunidad*. For example, it is common to refer to ethnic groups in such ways as El Pueblo Shuar or El Pueblo Kichwa and simultaneously refer to specific villages as "comunidades" when an emphasis on ethnic difference is implied. Key to this is the political nature of the use of the term *el pueblo*. Whitten (2003a:13) notes that the determination of who belongs to "el pueblo" is context-specific, and its use implies the "dynamic collective of 'the people.'" In some contexts this takes the form of nationalism, while in others "el pueblo" can refer to a specific group. For example, El Pueblo Ecuatoriano refers to the Ecuadorian people in a nationalistic sense, whereas El Pueblo Kichwa makes reference to a specific ethnic identity. El Consejo de Desarrollo de las Nacionalidades y Pueblos del Ecuador (CODENPE) most strongly illustrates the semantic relationship between el pueblo and indigeneity. Established in 1998, CODENPE supports development in accordance with Indigenous comunidades or pueblos. Thus, the use of the term *comunidad* as opposed to *comuna* is political. Comunidad indexes indigeneity whereas comuna does not.

María, a middle-aged mother from Salango, noted the significance of the adoption of a rhetoric emphasizing el pueblo and la comunidad when I spoke with her in 2016. María is small in stature, even by Ecuadorian standards, and her intelligence and insight are hidden behind her quiet demeanor. "Everything

FIGURE 4.1. *Doorway of the casa comunal*

changed when they adopted the idea of el pueblo, la comunidad," she lamented.
I asked what she meant. "They quickly changed from comuna to pueblo or
comunidad...it is now Pueblo Manta...Comunidad Salango. They have more
control now." "Why more control," I questioned. She paused in thought for a
moment and responded, "They control the [development] projects and what
happens. It is a small group, but they have control. It is no longer la comuna, it
is el pueblo and la comunidad." María did not identify any formal change in
power. In fact, the comuna still existed as an entity, but the casa comunal was
now painted with the words "Comunidad Salango" and "Pueblo Manta," along
with being adorned with symbols representative of pre-Columbian iconogra-
phy. What she did recognize is that the change in language was meaningful
and indicated a shift in local politics, power, and control.

PLURINATIONALISM AND THE POLITICS OF INCLUSION

The dynamic process of identity formation that occurred in Salango cannot
be understood fully without referencing significant changes that took place
in Ecuador at the level of state politics between 1990 and 2010. The changes
that will be addressed here are related directly to the political positioning of
CONAIE within Ecuador and the development of a national Indigenous
movement throughout the 1990s and early 2000s.

Whereas the case of Salango might seem localized, it is linked to a much broader set of national and international political constructs. The most prominent include the ratification of the International Labour Organization's (ILO's) Indigenous and Tribal Peoples Convention (ILO Convention no. 169) and the legal adoption of multiculturalism and, later, plurinationalism as underlying concepts of Indigenous and state political ideology. In what follows I suggest that the political shifts foreshadowed by the levantamiento indígena of 1990 resulted in structural and organizational changes to the centuries-old ethno-racial paradigm of mestizaje.

The case of Salango presents questions about the very nature of mestizaje and its meanings within Ecuador's current political climate while simultaneously lending insight into how notions of a homogeneous mestizo national identity are challenged from both above, through constitutional reform and an emphasis on plurinationalism, and below, through local-level ethno-political activism. The ratification of ILO Convention no. 169 and the legal adoption of multiculturalism and plurinationalism as underlying concepts of leftist Ecuadorian political ideology are critical for understanding Salango, as well as developing a broader perspective on mestizaje and ethnic politics in Ecuador. Convention 169 was established in 1989 and aims to ensure rights for Indigenous and tribal populations and to protect such populations as members of nation-states. As applied to Latin America and the case of mestizaje, Convention 169 challenges homogenization by calling on states to recognize diversity and equality.

A relevant note with regard to Convention 169 is that it does not attempt to define what constitutes Indigenous or tribal status. Instead, it specifically references *self-identification* as the key condition for establishing Indigenous identity. World Bank and UN definitions of what it means to be Indigenous follow the same criterion (Canessa 2006:242). With this in mind, standards outlined by the ILO for asserting an Indigenous identity include having a traditional lifestyle and cultural practices that differ from other segments of the national population, having ancestral ties to territory, having historical continuity, and having distinct social and political organizations (ILO Convention no. 169, Article 1). Convention 169 also recognizes the right of Indigenous and tribal peoples to "enjoy the full measure of human rights and fundamental freedoms without hindrance or discrimination" (ILO Convention no. 169, Article 3, no. 1).

With growing political pressure from CONAIE, Ecuador ratified Convention 169 on May 15, 1998, and drafted a new constitution corresponding to the convention's requirements that same year. The 1998 constitution defines

Ecuador as a multiethnic and multicultural state while also recognizing Indigenous rights and communities as *self-defined* nationalities (Constitución Política de la República del Ecuador 1998, Title III, chapter 5, Article 83).

The legislative changes of 1998 proved to be a symbolic victory for Indigenous peoples, but the political struggle for equal citizenship rights and the recognition of Indigenous culture as a valued component of Ecuadorian national identity continued even after the adoption of the 1998 constitution. One of the most notable features of post-1998 Indigenous politics in Ecuador was the push for legal recognition of the country as a plurinational state, a change that did not come until the drafting of the 2008 constitution (see Constitución Política de la República del Ecuador 2008). Selverston-Scher makes a case for a plurinational state as

> a type of social contract in which subgroups agree to sacrifice their autonomy in exchange for the economic, social, and political benefits they receive from sharing a state. The agreement can be entered into by force, by consent, by formal agreement, or tacitly. However, when the state becomes overtly loyal to one group over another or when some groups' expectations are not met, these marginalized groups may have cause to break the contract. The state has the responsibility of providing an incentive for its member groups to remain within the contract. The groups have the responsibility to support the functioning of the state. (Selverston-Scher 2001:20)

CONAIE approaches plurinationalism from the perspective of self-determination, autonomy, and inclusion (Confederación de Nacionalidades Indígenas del Ecuador 2007).[10] In addition, CONAIE makes specific reference to plurinationalism as related to discrimination, decolonization, and the challenging of racism:

> The plurinational state is a model of political organization for the decolonization of our nations and communities. It recognizes not only the contributions of the indigenous nationalities and communities to patrimony and cultural diversity, politics and civilizing of Ecuador, but looks to overcome centuries of poverty and discrimination of indigenous civilizations. The communities and nationalities for their sociocultural distinctions, politics and history demand specific rights . . . Plurinationalism will strengthen the new State, through consolidation of the unity in diversity and destroying the mode of racism. (Confederación de Nacionalidades Indígenas del Ecuador 2007:6, 10)[11]

In sum, plurinationalism in the case of Ecuador can be understood as state recognition of management of territory and resources by Indigenous communities and equal inclusion of Indigenous participants in the political process (Gutiérrez Chong 2010:264). Plurinationalism is not just the recognition of diversity but a declaration of empowerment that seeks to overcome centuries of racism and discrimination while challenging the ideology of mestizaje.

CONTEXTUALIZING THE CASE OF SALANGO

Taking into account ILO Convention 169 and the recognition of self-identification, territorial ties, and historical continuity as appropriate criteria for claims to Indigenous identity, one can begin to better understand the process of articulating an Indigenous identity, as reflected in the case of Pueblo Manta. The fact that ILO Convention 169 recognizes Indigenous communities as *self-defined* entities is essential to analyzing this process. For Manta communities, Indigenous identity is self-defined with reference to an archaeological record. Lending additional support to claims to Manta identity are ancestral ties to territory. Murra (1963) notes that Manta communities were mentioned in the writings of Spanish explorer Bartolomé Ruíz, and the name Manta was attributed to the trading peoples of the region. A contemporary symbol of the connection to the past is the well-known balsa raft, a symbol featured prominently in the local museum as well as in a painting by a local artist that hangs in a local restaurant. A similar image of the painting, by the same artist, is displayed on the cover of this book. The imagery provides a contemporary depiction of a prominent feature of early colonial encounters with the Manta. Murra (1963:804) provides this description: "All observers seem to agree that the maritime peoples of Manabí were great sailors, skillfully handling dug-out canoes and elaborate balsa rafts on fishing, commercial, or ceremonial trips . . . The large raft, equipped with sails and cabin, carrying some 20 people and 30 tons of merchandise, met by Bartolomé Ruíz gives an idea of the extent and magnitude of coastwise traffic undertaken by these people . . . When captured, its Indian crew said they came from Calangane, which [Paul] Rivet and [Jacinto] Jijón locate in Manabí."

The history documented by Murra (1963) is something that is not overlooked by local residents. Coupled with the archaeological record, such accounts provide the basis for contemporary claims about ethnic identity. Prehistory and archaeology are such significant features in defining contemporary Pueblo Manta communities that the 2005 petition to CODENPE for state recognition as an Indigenous community references archaeology in four of the sixteen points. In addition, history, territory, and ancestry are prominent themes when it comes to defining Manta identity (Pueblo Manta 2005).

The influence of CONAIE can be seen in the organization of the Pueblo Manta document into sixteen points, and the petition presented by Pueblo Manta corresponds to the guidelines put forth in ILO Convention 169 by self-identifying Indigenous identity, referencing historical continuity in a certain area (e.g., a connection to territory), and suggesting unique cultural elements that distinguish Pueblo Manta from other segments of society. In addition, founding documents of Pueblo Manta emphasize territory as key to identity by referencing the "conservation and administration of ancestral lands" as one of the main objectives (Pueblo Manta 2005, Article 5, no. 1). This parallels the focus of CONAIE's original sixteen points presented in 1990 as part of the levantamiento indígena, which emphasize identity and cultural issues including land rights (see Yashar 2005 for a detailed discussion). The Pueblo Manta focus on archaeology also corresponds to the original sixteen points set forth by CONAIE and the explicit mention of the protection of archaeological sites (Beck and Mijeski 2011:37; Yashar 2005:146). All of these elements align with the criteria for asserting an Indigenous identity established in Convention 169.

As noted by Hale (1997), new articulations of identity, such as the case of Salango, require a delicate balance between claims to continuity that are imbued with a sense of timelessness (primordialism) and claims that are instrumental and that only emerge through an organized effort to promote change. This corresponds directly to the work of Sandstrom (2008) and the recognition that instrumentalism and primordialism, often constructed, are not mutually exclusive. What I have suggested thus far is that while the assertion of Manta identity is a recent phenomenon, claims to identity emphasize a perceived continuity that has a basis in material connections to the archaeological record as well as to the natural environment or commons. In particular, locals assert a connection to the past by way of economic engagement in the form of work related to the ocean, where fishing and diving are practiced in the present while also dating back 5,000 years. Beyond these considerations, the emergence of Manta identity as a legally recognized identity is a product of changes in laws and the legal adoption of Convention 169 and constitutional recognition of plurinationalism. In this way Manta ethnogenesis corresponds to the case presented by French (2009) that addresses similar issues of identity in Brazil. A particularly relevant takeaway from French's analysis is that changes in laws often foster alternative perceptions about cultural practices and even new understandings of identity. Anderson (2007), Brondo (2010), and Latorre (2013) provide similar accounts from throughout Latin America, where legal changes and the adoption of multiculturalism and plurinational-ism create a space for debate about the meanings of identity categories while also providing a space for the emergence of "new" identities. In the case of Salango, economic practice and the archaeological record have historically informed local understandings of identity. However, the legal changes associated with Convention 169 and plurinationalism fostered alternative understandings of identity while still emphasizing continuity.

MEANINGS AND CONTESTATION

Even as Salango gained recognition as an Indigenous community, the meanings attributed to Manta identity have not become uniform, and my experiences with residents indicate a degree of ambiguity about what it means to be Manta. Moreover, a notable discrepancy between collective and individual understandings of identity points to the untidy and heterogeneous nature of identity in Pueblo Manta communities as well as the complexities of race and ethnicity in Ecuador.

Part of this project, referenced as well in a previous article (Bauer 2012), took the form of an extensive survey and interviews conducted on various research trips to Salango between 2009 and 2013. Even though I had witnessed the changes taking place in Salango, prior to 2009 most of my research was qualitative. I wanted to gain a more quantitative perspective and expand my research by including a different methodological approach. While my intentions may have been somewhat selfish, I also thought a quantitative approach would provide different results than had the purely qualitative approach I previously employed. Not only was my intent to have something more quantifiable, I also desired to gain insight into how residents perceived of and responded to the designation of the community as an Indigenous community. Was there a shared understanding of what it means to be Manta? How did local residents make sense of this designation? My sense at the time was that the designation would mean different things to different people and that while it held deep meaning for the comuna and for local politics, it might not be so important for community residents. Moreover, I was interested in finding out if the collective identity of Manta corresponded to the individual identities expressed by community members. The methodology for this portion of the research was fairly straightforward. I gathered data based on a total of 151 surveys conducted in Salango and the neighboring village of Río Chico (also part of the comuna Salango). Ninety women and sixty-one men participated in the survey, and participants ranged in age from eighteen to eighty-five.

Multiple factors were taken into consideration in the formulation of the survey, including demographic information such as sex, age, place of birth, occupation,

ETHNIC IDENTIFIER							
	Mestizo	Cholo	Moreno	Montubio	Zambo	Indígena	Other
SEX							
Male	25	19	2	5	1	0	9
Female	47	29	2	1	1	1	9
Total	72	48	4	6	2	1	18

FIGURE 4.2. *Summary data of self-identification. The terms in the survey table represent the common ethno-racial folk taxonomy of Ecuador. Mestizo refers to individuals of mixed Indigenous and European descent. Cholo is a term utilized on the coast to refer to peasant fishermen. It also contains negative connotations associated with being lower class. However, the term is also embraced by many residents of rural coastal Ecuador. Moreno refers to dark-skinned individuals, often exhibiting phenotypic contributions of African descent. Montubio refers to coastal peasants of mixed descent and carries the negative connotations of ignorant and backward. Like the term cholo, it is often used with pride by many coastal-dwelling individuals. Zambo refers to an individual of mixed African and Indigenous or mestizo descent. Indígena refers to Indigenous descent.*

and ethnicity. Consultants were also asked to provide their perspectives on the recent designation of the comuna as Pueblo Manta. In addition, respondents were asked whether they were registered members of the comuna.

The results of the surveys and associated interviews provide insights into local conceptions of identity in Salango. The first thing that becomes clear from the data is that the majority of the respondents did not identify as Manta or Indigenous but self-identified as mestizo or *cholo*. This contrasts with what might be expected from a community that recently gained Indigenous status. Explanations are multiple. One potential explanation is that respondents were not forthcoming about their identity and that the survey results are therefore not an accurate reflection of peoples' conceptions of individual identity. This is always a challenge in ethnographic research, but we must work to make sense of the data we have. Related to this explanation and perhaps lending clarity to it is the suggestion that the politics of mestizaje still influence the way people self-identify individually, and the centuries of oppression and marginalization of Indigenous peoples make it challenging or perhaps awkward for people to claim an Indigenous identity. In fact, data from Ecuador's 2010 census compare closely with the data presented in this study. In Manabí province, less than 1 percent of respondents self-identified as Indigenous in the 2010 national census (Gobierno del Ecuador n.d.). This figure varies only slightly from the 2001 census.

Martínez Novo (2014) provides a detailed analysis of the complexities of Ecuador's national census results from 2010. She traces changes in the census from a focus on documentation for the sake of taxation to a focus on nationalism and mestizaje to an era of civil rights and Indigenous movements. Martínez Novo suggests that the 2010 census reflects indigeneity in a particular way, and that is why the results indicate an Indigenous population of only 7.0 percent in 2010 as opposed to 16.3 percent in 1950. At issue is the framing and type of questions asked on the census. Prior to 1950, race was used for taxation purposes. In 1950 the census used language. In 2001 the census adopted a form of self-identification that emphasized race by asking people to identify as Indigenous, black (Afro-Ecuadorian), white, mestizo, mulatto, or other. The 2010 census made a transition from race to ethnicity by framing the question with regard to "culture and customs" (Martínez Novo 2014:407). The challenge then becomes how to make sense of the complex interpretations of race and ethnicity. Whereas a focus on language can provide some clarity, there are challenges in disentangling the concepts of race and ethnicity. The two concepts, their meanings, and how they are expressed are untidy and prone to interpretation.

When the lens is shifted to collective identity, something different becomes evident. In 1989 only three Indigenous ethnic groups were recognized as residing in Ecuador's five coastal provinces (Pallares 2002:6–7). In 2014 there were six recognized Indigenous ethnic groups in those same five provinces (CONAIE n.d.). I suggest that the structural changes in the form of the ratification of Convention 169 and the official adoption of plurinationalism are in part responsible for the increase in recognition of Indigenous groups on the Ecuadorian coast.

Returning to the data from Salango on self-identification, individuals often neglected to respond directly to the question on ethno-racial identification. Among both males and females, some did not respond to the question or provided answers that deviated from those given in the survey. Answers that deviated most often linked people to their native communities, and people claimed an identity related to territory and community as opposed to one associated with a specific ethno-racial category. For example, "I am Salangueño" or "I am Manaba" were common responses. Specific to this is the phrase "Hijo del pueblo" (child of the village), which is commonplace throughout Salango and surrounding communities and is also present in the song "Salango Lindo" (chapter 2).

Qualitative data taken from the surveys and interviews provide additional insight into resident conceptions of identity. Elsa, a forty-one-year-old female resident, spoke about Manta identity thus: "It is good because it is a way of identifying ourselves." Implicit in this statement is that identifying as Pueblo Manta establishes difference through the assertion of an Indigenous identity that contrasts with any homogenized form of mestizo identity. Of note is that Elsa self-identified as mestiza but favored Manta identity in terms of thinking about a collective identity. Similarly, a thirty-five-year-old female resident who identified as mestiza asserted that adopting an Indigenous designation allows people to "know their origins." In this case it would appear that indigeneity was associated with ancestry or race and not necessarily with ethnicity. Consultants also made references to the past to establish a discourse of continuity. One individual stated "we are from ancestral roots," while another showed support for the Indigenous designation: "It is okay because before, our ancestors lived here." Again, the issue is ancestry and not necessarily an ethnic (culturally based) identity.

The 2006 designation of Salango as an Indigenous community seems to be at odds with local conceptions of individual ethnic identity. However, despite not self-identifying as Indigenous, there is a strong tendency for residents to reference collective identity with regard to indigeneity or at least regarding the Indigenous past and the archaeological record (Bauer 2010b, 2014; Hernández-Ramírez and Ruiz-Ballesteros 2011; Rowe 2012). For example, during conversations with local residents, it was common to hear references to having ancestral roots or to ancestors as Indigenous. This corresponds directly with the documents put forth by Pueblo Manta in petitioning for government recognition of a collective Indigenous identity. Specifically, the *Estatuto del Pueblo Manta* (2005:Article 1) references Pueblo Manta as "a historic organization of ancestral roots, descendants of the Manteño."[12] This is comparable to the work of Briones (2003:37), in which "Mapuche identities are nurtured by images that picture not only a proud continuity between ancestors and descendants, but also a troublesome continuity, endangered by critical gaps." The Manteño were contacted by the Spanish in the 1520s, and the positioning of Pueblo Manta as a "historic organization" matches Murra's (1963:803) description of the organization of Ecuador's coast at the time of Spanish contact—a description that references multiple contemporary Pueblo Manta communities. However, for many residents of those communities, as with the case of the Mapuche presented by Briones, there is a degree of discontinuity that makes it plausible for residents of Manta communities to question the efficacy of indigeneity as a concept applied to contemporary residents.

CONCLUSION

Ecuador's ratification of ILO Convention 169 and related changes, including the adoption of a new constitution in 1998 and again in 2008, left an indelible mark on Indigenous politics. Beyond the highland and Amazonian Indigenous movements and the politics of CONAIE and its political arm, *Pachakutik Nuevo País*, the formal political processes outlined in this chapter have fundamentally altered the structure of mestizaje in Ecuador by expanding opportunities for representation beyond the scope of groups traditionally recognized as Indigenous.[13] With these changes come questions regarding the very nature of indigeneity and its multiple meanings. As my research indicates, the concept of indigeneity is not fixed, and it is clearly context-dependent. Moreover, while it can be argued that the constitutional adoption of plurinationalism has resulted in a more inclusive Ecuador, the country is still informed by the legacy of mestizaje and the politics of exclusion.

There are numerous issues to address with reference to the rise of identity-based politics in Salango. First, there exists a clear connection between territorial rights and emerging Indigenous social movements (see Brondo 2010 and Latorre 2013 for additional examples). In the case of Salango, the adoption of an ethnic discourse provided local residents with greater leverage in negotiating with the state, largely because of the long history of Indigenous politics in Ecuador. While the conflict in Salango was a conflict over land, it was equally a conflict over development and the community's ability to control the appropriate course of development. Perhaps most important, the conflict was about identity and the self-assertion of ethnicity.

The dynamic process of ethnogenesis in Salango was the result of dissatisfaction with the state-sponsored establishment of a rigid classificatory system that makes it difficult for non-Indigenous populations to lay claim to traditionally held territories. Biord (2006) discusses territoriality with reference to ethnogenesis and maintains that claims to territory consist of more than rights to a physical space but also include a space in which community is produced, the type of space outlined by Gudeman (2001) in his discussion of community economics and discussed in chapter 2 of this volume. The suggestion here is that territory has a value that extends beyond its mere physicality. Biord's (2006) reference to the cultural value of territory, while different contextually from any of the claims made by Gudeman (2001), can be related to what Gudeman refers to as the "shared value" of the commons. A critical feature of Gudeman's (2001:27) discussion is his assertion that the commons is "the patrimony or legacy of a community . . . anything that contributes to the material and social sustenance of a people with a shared identity." When access to territory is denied or rights to territory are negated, the legacy of a community is transformed. In related form, Brondo asserts that "history making" involves establishing a narrative about a presence within the landscape and a connection to territory. This is done by recounting stories that help "make place" by referencing tradition, use, and attachment to territory (Brondo 2010:182). These elements are represented clearly in the way Salangueños reference their relationship to place. Moreover, it is evident that Salangueños conceive of their identity as well as their belonging to a community with reference to territory.

While questions of land and development are central features of the growth of Indigenous politics in Salango, identity is also at the core of the case presented in this chapter. Hill and Wilson (2003) suggest that identities are constantly undergoing processes of negotiation and that social scientists are well-informed to examine the political dimensions of identity. The recent growth of groups that define their identity based on common heritage and shared ethnicity exemplifies the fluid and often seemingly unbounded nature of ethnicity. As Hall asserts, "Perhaps instead of thinking of identity as an already accomplished fact, which the new cultural practices then represent, we should think, instead, of identity as a 'production' which is never complete, always in process, and always constituted within, not outside[,] representation" (Hall 1990:222). It is the task of scholars to examine the social relations that result in identity production or the formation of ethnic groups (Banks 1996) by focusing not only on how traditions, ethnic or otherwise, are created but instead by asking why, or in response to what, traditions are created (Thomas 1992). Salango provides a definitive case for referencing not only how but why ethnic discourses emerge. The success of Indigenous organizations including CONAIE at the national level and MIPMAWPU on the Ecuadorian coast provided a valuable opening for groups not historically recognized as Indigenous to stake claim to an Indigenous identity.

Another dimension worth considering is the complexity of race and ethnicity and how these terms are expressed and understood by locals. Drawing on the work of Martínez Novo (2014:407) and recognizing that "race and ethnicity cannot be neatly distinguished theoretically," it is also true that there are challenges to the practical task of distinguishing race and ethnicity, especially as they relate to people's conceptions about identity. In the individual responses from my own survey work, it appears as though people were responding in terms of what they perceive to be their ethnic identity. They emphasized culture, in part because they are not readily discernible from other people and groups along the coast who are monolingual in Spanish, who practice Catholicism and other Christian religious traditions, and who are generally regarded as peasants who survive on a mixed subsistence strategy of fishing and horticulture. However, at the same time, the issue of ancestry (race) is worth mentioning. Indigeneity for many people in Salango is associated with ancestry or race but is not necessarily a component of their sense of ethnicity. Perhaps it is then the case that Salangueños identify ethnically as mestizo, montubio, or cholo while still recognizing the contribution of Indigenous ancestry and race. However, when it becomes advantageous or only at discrete moments, ancestry is parlayed into an expression of ethnic identity.

In addition to the aforementioned considerations, I suggest that we can explain the lack of identification as Indigenous and the more common reference to self-identity as mestizo or montubio by thinking about identity and belonging. What I am proposing, following the line of thought of Barth (1998), is that indigeneity corresponds to boundary making or designating difference. Thus, Salangueño claims to an Indigenous identity distinguish Salango and associated Pueblo Manta communities from the majority of other communities throughout the region. For residents of Salango, self-identification overwhelmingly reflects belonging—"experiences of being part of the social fabric . . . and emotional inclusion" (Anthias 2008:8)—whether as mestizo, montubio, Salangueño, Manaba, or "un hijo del pueblo." This stands in marked contrast to the politicized Manta identity. Thus, collective versus individual conceptions of identity are heavily dependent on political motivations and a process of establishing boundaries through the assertion of ethnic difference.

In chapter 5 I explore the consequences of the recently adopted Manta identity for development and the local economy. In doing so, I argue that identity became a mechanism for negotiating development practices and maintaining political control within the context of continuity and change.

NOTES

1. A previous version of this chapter was published in the *Bulletin of Latin American Research* (see Bauer 2010a).

2. *Ethnic Groups and Boundaries: The Social Organization of Cultural Difference* is a volume edited by Fredrik Barth (1998) and is considered one of the most significant works relating to ethnic identity formation. It stands out as one of the earliest writings to emphasize relations of power as central to understanding ethnic identities.

3. The encomienda system persisted in Ecuador throughout the colonial period. It was defined by land and labor being granted to Spanish colonizers in exchange for their willingness to defend their territory and oversee religious indoctrination of the Indigenous population. Reducciones were Indigenous settlements that were established by the colonial regime to provide better oversight and control over payment of Indigenous tribute, religious conversation, and labor.

4. Gonzales and González suggest that autonomy can be conceived of in terms of both individual citizenship rights as well as a means for "transforming colonizing practices that are embedded in the state" (Gonzales and González 2015:2).

5. The term *nationality* (*nacionalidad*) is used throughout Ecuador to refer to specific Indigenous ethnic groups. It is also common for Indigenous groups to use the word *pueblo* as a self-referential term.

6. The Amazonian provinces of Morona, Napo, Pastaza, Sucumbíos, and Zamora claim a total Indigenous population of 22 percent, while the highland provinces of Azuay, Bolivar, Cañar, Carchi, Chimborazo, Cotopaxi, Imbabura, Loja, Pichincha, and Tungurahua boast a combined Indigenous population of 28 percent (Van Cott 2005).

7. Montubio has the alternate spelling montuvio.

8. Wankavilka has the alternate spelling Huancavilca. The website is Inec.gov.ec.

9. La CONAIE rechaza la intervención del señor Patrick Bredthauer y solidariza con la comunidad Salango para que sus derechos de vivir en paz y desarrollo comunitario de acuerdo a sus formas de vida continua y exige el gobierno central garantizar que la comunidad ancestral de Salango sea de exclusiva competencia del CODENPE (Macas 2007).

10. As noted by Moreno Parra and Machado Maturana (2001:74), autonomy refers to the right to self-jurisdiction as compatible with cultural values. Thus, autonomy does not mean separation from the state but rather the ability to control one's own destiny and to maintain cultural traditions. Ibarra (1996) and Cruz Rodríguez (2012) highlight self-administration of territory and decentralization as fundamental components of CONAIE's push for Indigenous autonomy.

11. El estado plurinacional es un modelo de organización política para la descolonización de nuestras naciones y pueblos. Es reconocer no solamente el aporte de los pueblos y nacionalidades indígenas al patrimonio de la diversidad cultural, política y civilizatoria del Ecuador, sino que buscar superar el empobrecimiento y la discriminación de siglos de las civilizaciones indígenas. Los pueblos y nacionalidades por sus peculiaridades socioculturales, políticas e históricas reclaman derechos específicos y que son aportes como valores simbólicos, formas de ejercicio de la autoridad y sistemas de administración social de enorme mérito y valor político . . . La plurinacionalidad fortalecerá al nuevo Estado, mediante la consolidación de la unidad en la diversidad, destruyendo de este modo el racismo (Confederación de Nacionalidades Indígenas del Ecuador 2007:6, 10).

12. El pueblo Manta, es una entidad histórica y de raíces ancestrales, descendientes de los Manteños (Estatuto del Pueblo Manta 2005:Article 1).

13. Pachakutik Nuevo País (Movement for Plurinational Unity) was established in 1995 and is the political party associated with CONAIE. The word *pachakutik* is an Indigenous Kichwa term that refers to inversion or turning over (Becker 2008).

5

Diego said he wanted to talk to me about a boat.[1] He brought the topic to my attention along with Manuel when the two of them invited me to join them at a small café in Puerto López. I learned throughout my time in the field that such invitations, either to go out to eat or for a formal meal in a family's home, usually signified the inevitability of a serious conversation that was often tied to a request. I also became aware that I was viewed as a source of knowledge about tourism, and it was fairly normal for Diego and Manuel as well as other community members to ask for my advice and share their ideas with me. Individuals with whom I did not have a close relationship would often pass their requests on to Manuel or Diego and use them as intermediaries to convey the requests. The relationship of requests was a normal part of the relationship of *compadrazgo* I established with Manuel when I accepted the invitation to be the padrino of his oldest son. My relationship with Manuel and his family would forever be changed as a consequence, as would the obligations we would have to one another.

Manuel, Diego, and I sat at a small table on the second-floor balcony that overlooked the beach. A large bottle of Pilsener perspired as Diego filled three small glasses about halfway with the light, crisp beer that is a symbol of Ecuadorian national identity. "Drink up, *mi pana*," he said while raising his glass to the middle of the table for the ritual *salud* (salutation) that is pronounced before drinking. The cool (not cold) beer passed easily

DOI: 10.5876/9781607327608.c005

across my lips as the late morning sun foreshadowed an unseasonably hot day. "*Compa*, we have a question to ask you," Manuel stated with a formality that was not a normal part of our interactions. "We have talked a lot and we want to buy a boat ... a boat for tourism." "We think it is a good idea. Look here, in Puerto López, tourism is growing. There are lots of opportunities in Salango," Diego chimed in as he often did to try to reinforce the message presented by Manuel. Despite the formality of the conversation, it was little more than a request for advice and consultation. And so it would begin, a foray into tourism for two of my closest confidants in Salango and two of my closest friends in life.

This chapter deals with tourism in Salango. In keeping with the general theme of continuity and change, I focus on tourism as a significant change being experienced by Salangueños while also suggesting that identity in its various forms is fundamental to an understanding of tourism development in Salango. Local development processes are conceived of with reference to the various manifestations of identity outlined in the previous chapters. In some cases identity is an explicit component of development processes; in other instances identity is only loosely connected to development practices. I provide three brief cases of tourism development in Salango, all of which were taking place at various times from 2002 to the present. I focus on a non-governmental organization (NGO)–supported tourism cooperative that began in 2002, community-organized and World Bank–funded tourism that was initiated in 2006, and independent tourism development that began that same year. The questions that guide this chapter include understanding how identity influences development practices, analyzing how local-level development relates to national and global development discourses, and examining what I refer to as development politics and the politics of development. Drawing from the work of Hill and Wilson (2003) on identity politics and the politics of identities, I conceive of development politics as the ways development is promoted and negotiated with reference to powerful agents of change, including the state, NGOs, and international development organizations. Politics of development is here conceived of as the strategic use of politics and frames of understanding by local populations during the process of development. I argue that by adopting a perspective that highlights the politics of development, we can gain a deeper appreciation for the challenges and complexities of rural development practices.

TOURISM AS DEVELOPMENT

Tropical regions of the world are often targeted for tourism development, and in many cases tourism is promoted as a viable alternative to natural resource exploitation and extractive activities that are deemed environmentally damaging and unsustainable. Tourism in Salango fits within this general trend and is in part a response to declining fisheries production and a need for local residents to seek economic alternatives. The Ecuadorian government has made a concerted effort to promote tourism within the country as well as abroad. One notable example includes spending US$3.8 million to purchase thirty seconds of commercial air time during Super Bowl 49, which aired on February 1, 2015. The commercial, playing to the tune of the Beatles classic "All You Need Is Love," was part of Ecuador's "All You Need Is Ecuador" tourism campaign and was the first time a foreign country purchased advertising time to promote tourism during the Super Bowl.

Tourism is big business, and the Ecuadorian government has done a great deal to promote it. Statistics from Ecuador's Ministry of Tourism indicate that tourism has nearly doubled since 2006, with foreign entries into Ecuador by tourists growing from 799,080 individuals in 2006 to 1,480,970 in 2014 (Ministerio de Turismo n.d.a; Ministerio de Turismo n.d.b). During the same period the number of visitors to Manabí's Machalilla National Park increased from 34,829 to 224,559 (Ministerio de Turismo n.d.a; Ministerio de Turismo n.d.b). Infrastructural improvements, such as the opening of new international airports in both Guayaquil and Quito and the rebuilding of Highway E15 to improve access to Ecuador's coastal provinces, are partly responsible for the growth of tourism under President Rafael Correa. Elected in 2006, Correa's campaign strategy relied heavily on his assertion that tourism would be the future of Ecuador. This message was presented in October 2006 when he visited Puerto López during a brief campaign stop on the Manabí coast. Speaking to a raucous crowd that packed the main street leading to the malecón, Correa championed tourism as the future of Manabí. In particular, he spoke out against environmentally destructive practices such as petroleum extraction (his position later changed) and the declining fishing industry along the coast, including in Salango and Puerto López.

A rhetoric of change was in the air, not only in the words spoken by Correa but also in the eyes of many in Salango. Meetings about tourism were becoming increasingly common, and little by little people were starting to view tourism as an alternative to the dominant fishing and diving economy. "Tourism is the future. Fishing is more and more difficult, but with tourism we have options," commented a young diver who was working to make the transition from diving to tourism. Not all perspectives were as optimistic, however. As Javier commented in a conversation in 2003:

Everything happens little by little. The people need to look in a different direction. Fishing is life, but it is poor. People need to look elsewhere. I want to see change. I want the village to improve. Many people are twenty, thirty, eighty years old. Eighty is the same as twenty, same work, same bed, more children, more hunger. People are comfortable. They live for fishing. They don't believe that they can live without fishing. Tourism allows us to use what we know . . . we are fishermen and divers, and tourism uses the same resource that we have used for generations.

The focus on continuity is an element detailed further in the forthcoming discussion of tourism development. However, for the moment, what is essential is the recognition that ideas about tourism are present both nationally and locally. If we take into consideration Ecuador's promotion of tourism during the Super Bowl, we might even say there is a global connection. Central to understating tourism in Salango is examining the process by which tourism is negotiated and how local ideas and practices relating to tourism, as a form of development, link to the broader perspective nationally and beyond. Moreover, it is relevant to understand the struggles of residents of Salango as they have attempted to engage in tourism. The case studies presented in this chapter illustrate that while tourism has increased significantly in Ecuador from 2006 to the present, the benefits have not always been felt by the residents of rural communities where tourism is increasingly becoming a daily reality.

CASE STUDY ONE: NGO-SPONSORED DEVELOPMENT AND THE POLITICS OF A TOURISM COOPERATIVE

When I first met Manuel in 2002, he shared his participation in a local tourism cooperative known as PARCEMAR. Established in 2002, the name PARCEMAR comes from the phrase *parcela marina* (marine plot) and references the establishment of a protected area just north of the beach of Isla Salango. Tourism in Salango takes various forms but is predominantly focused on the ocean and includes activities such as snorkeling, whale watching, and sport fishing excursions. Whale watching corresponds to the annual migration of humpback whales past the coast of Ecuador during the months of June through September, and it is such a prominent part of tourism along the Ecuadorian coast that the town of Puerto López is the self-proclaimed "Whale Watching Capital of the World." PARCEMAR sought to take advantage of these activities while providing economic opportunities to people already familiar with the ocean.

The creation of the cooperative was part of a project supported by the Committee for the Development of the Peoples (CISP), a European NGO that provides funds for environmental conservation efforts. It is fairly common for conservation to be coupled with tourism development efforts (see Buckley 2010), and NGOs often play a vital role in the process of implementing conservation-based development projects. This is true in Ecuador, as NGOs are viewed as having the capacity to work closely with local communities while executing projects in a timely manner when the state does not have the resources or expertise (Segarra 1997). Thus, NGOs often serve as outside agents that negotiate projects at the local level while meeting state development goals in areas beyond the reach of the state apparatus. Indeed, an entire development economy has emerged with the growth of NGOs in the 1980s; globally, billions of US dollars flow through NGOs annually as they work to promote development efforts. A frequent result is that NGOs themselves develop the same inefficient bureaucracies they were designed to avoid.

PARCEMAR began with an original membership of seven divers. Diving is a dangerous and unpredictable activity, perhaps even more than fishing. Similar to Herlihy's (2012) detailed ethnography of divers in coastal Honduras, the divers of Salango experience high levels of uncertainty and danger, and to be a diver is to be respected. Divers are akin to North American notions of cowboys in the Wild West. Diving is a macho activity. It runs through family lines of men who are independent and a bit rough and who in the earliest days of my research held a prominent social position in Salango. Divers like Manuel, Diego, Mario, and others were regarded as tough young men who risked their lives to provide for their families. They would travel long distances and sometimes reap high rewards, more than the average fisherman in Salango could imagine.

As opposed to the fishermen of Salango who work the coastal waters not far from the mainland, divers gained a substantial part of their annual income during the relatively short (two- to three-month) *pepino* (sea cucumber) and *langosta* (lobster) seasons that occurred with varying frequency in the Galapagos Islands. The most notable boom in pepino harvesting was between 1996 and 2002, when the documented harvest increased from 38 metric tons to 176 metric tons (Shepherd et al. 2004). I recall the earliest years of my research, when the majority of the young divers of Salango would leave for the Galapagos in late June to work in difficult conditions and come back a few months later, often with hefty sums of money and numerous newly purchased commercial goods—including new clothes, tennis shoes, and watches. Manuel did just that. On one occasion he returned with two fishing rods and reels worth about US$1,200 each that he had purchased secondhand in the Galapagos with the intent of selling them for a profit on the mainland. As successful as diving was in the Galapagos, restrictions put in place limited diving to permanent residents of the islands, cracked down on illegal harvesting of pepino, and eliminated the opportunity for most Salango divers to take advantage of work there. In 2004 I said goodbye to Diego as he and his cousin Eduardo left Salango to head to Guayaquil to catch a plane to the Galapagos. They returned two days later, only to indicate that their contact in the Galapagos told them they would be unable to work because of the newly implemented restrictions. Neither has since gone back to the Galapagos.

Despite the substantial economic benefits of working in the Galapagos, often as much as $1,500 for two months' work compared to less than $400 earned on the mainland for the same amount of work, most divers resented working there. Stories ranged from enthusiastic accounts of the beauty and serenity of the islands, the abundance of wildlife, and the potential for fortune to stories of misery and fear as a result of exhausting work conditions and the dangers of working on the open ocean. Diving in the Galapagos meant spending two months aboard a 15 meter boat with as many as twenty other people. The divers ate and slept on the boat as it made its way to different dive sites in the waters surrounding the islands. Fibras were towed behind the larger boats. Each day, the divers would go out in a fibra, often spending six–eight hours below the surface of the Pacific Ocean while oxygen was pumped through a ½-inch-diameter tube by way of a gasoline-powered air compressor situated on the floor of the fibra high above the diver. The compressors are notorious for contaminating the oxygen that passes through the hose as gasoline and oil fumes are sucked in through the intake valve. Work is difficult and dangerous, and in the worst circumstances a diver can develop decompression sickness with no means of treatment prior to being flown to the mainland. Despite the good pay, many divers expressed a strong desire not to return to work in the Galapagos.

Divers were some of the earliest promoters of tourism in Salango. Because of their relative economic security and their lack of desire or inability to return to work in the Galapagos, divers have been much more apt than fishermen to view tourism as a viable economic alternative to marine resource extraction. Moreover, the relative independence of divers, who usually work in pairs as opposed to well-organized groups while in Salango, provided them with the freedom to explore economic opportunities other than diving. Whereas members of commercial fishing crews tend to be linked by strong kinship ties and a clear family history of fishing, with fishing crews consisting of five or more members, diving is much more individualistic. Divers also have much more free time to explore economic avenues other than diving, since diving is heavily reliant on water clarity, waves, and currents. Unlike the lunar cycle that is used for fishing, water clarity is highly unpredictable. It can vary from one day to the next and is dependent on wind and the condition of the ocean's currents. In times of even minimal wind and strong waves, divers are unable to dive. As a consequence of the erratic nature of weather patterns, divers often work as few as ten days per month. In addition, even while working close to home, the same dangers occur as those in the Galapagos. Diving is a young man's occupation, and most divers stop working in their early thirties. All of these factors result in a situation in which divers are much more likely to adopt tourism as an alternative to commercial diving while fishermen are less likely to engage in tourism activities.

With these factors in mind, PARCEMAR was formed. CISP worked with the members of the cooperative to institute an organizational structure that required each member of PARCEMAR to "buy in" to the cooperative by purchasing a share for US$50. CISP matched the funds, resulting in a total cost of US$100 per share. CISP also provided the members of PARCEMAR with items including life jackets and marine radios.

CISP representatives were no longer present in Salango when I arrived in 2002, but there was strong enthusiasm among the members of PARCEMAR, and it appeared that the idea of tourism was something to which the members were responsive. The positive outlook was in part a result of members' familiarity with the growing tourism industry in Puerto López and optimism that Salango could also develop into an important destination for tourists, albeit on a smaller scale. Moreover, most divers had a strong familiarity with tourism from their time spent in the Galapagos.

The organization of PARCEMAR allowed individual members to open their own tourism offices with the affiliation maintained with the cooperative. The initial plan was also for members to work together and share resources such as boats, life jackets, radios, and similar items. Within months of the implementation of the cooperative, two of the members of PARCEMAR opened their own small offices in Salango, and the other five members combined their resources to open a single office with the PARCEMAR namesake.

Membership in PARCEMAR grew from seven to twelve by 2004. Although efforts were made to increase the organization, a number of factors inhibited the growth and prosperity of the tourism cooperative. Startup costs were one reason PARCEMAR's success was limited. Members of PARCEMAR needed to outfit their boats and pay for guide licenses. At the time, only one boat in

Salango was a tourism boat. The other boats used for tourism were fishing fibras that were not appropriately equipped for tourism and were increasingly scrutinized under the watchful eye of park officials. Guide licenses allowing access to Machalilla National Park and Isla de la Plata cost US$100 per individual. Fees also needed to be paid to the municipal office in Puerto López to register PARCEMAR as a business. The total cost of fees to be paid to the municipality was US$120 in 2003, and members of PARCEMAR were also required to register with the regional tourism authority in Puerto López at an additional cost of US$64 annually.

In addition to the extensive financial output required to legally establish the tourism cooperative, regulations required that each boat used for tourism purposes have two motors. To add an additional motor to each of the boats in operation, the members of PARCEMAR determined that they would have to acquire nearly US$10,000. The overall startup cost quickly exceeded the initial amount invested by each member.

Funding was not the only problem PARCMEAR members encountered. During my time working with them, I frequently participated in conversations pertaining to the organization's relationship with Machalilla National Park. Many members shared the concern that the national park favored the tourism offices in Puerto López. Don Léon, a retired diver and a proponent of tourism in Salango, spoke of the relationship between PARCEMAR and the national park during a conversation outside his home:

> The problem with tourism here is that everything is associated with [Puerto] López and the national park. For example, if people want to have tours here in Salango and they want the tours to go to Isla de la Plata, they can't . . . They keep track of the visitors and once the maximum number of visitors is reached, no more are allowed. It also costs a lot of money and in order to have access to areas associated with the park, the tour company has to pay. The agencies in López have an advantage over us because the national park has an office in López. This office helps the agencies there but ignores the offices in Salango.

As the result of a perceived lack of support from the municipal government and the regional tourism authority, the members of PARCEMAR never acquired the requisite guide licenses for Machalilla National Park. The fact that they did not obtain those licenses greatly inhibited their chances of success. Whereas whale-watching tours near Isla Salango cost US$15 per person, Isla de la Plata is the destination most often frequented by tourists. Between January and July 2001, more than 6,300 tourists visited Isla de la Plata (Baquero 2002) at a cost of approximately US$40 per person. The inability of

PARCEMAR members to obtain licenses for Machalilla National Park was therefore a significant obstacle to the organization's growth and prosperity. The situation has continued in more recent years, with restrictions imposed by the park making it increasingly difficult for tourism operators in Salango to be successful. Some of these restrictions will be addressed later in this chapter.

Adding to the challenges associated with the park is the fact that despite promotion of tourism by the Ecuadorian government, it is difficult for small entrepreneurs to access the much-needed capital for local-level development initiatives. PARCEMAR members pointed to a lack of government assistance as one of the primary obstacles inhibiting the growth of the tourism cooperative. "People in Salango can't afford to pay, and there is no governmental assistance," lamented don León. Government loans are extremely difficult to obtain, and small-scale bank loans to entrepreneurs require substantial collateral. "There is no incentive [for tourism]. The government promotes tourism, but it also impedes progress. There is no form of [government] assistance. In Ecuador, the government just takes from the people. The money goes directly into the pockets of the rich. The rich get richer and the poor get poorer," don León stated with despair while running his finger across his throat. Funding represents an ongoing problem, and most tourism operators in Salango have to search for personal loans from friends or family or pool family resources to be competitive with the offices in Puerto López, which are supported predominantly by relatively wealthy investors from Quito, Guayaquil, and abroad. For example, in 2005 outside investors owned ten of the twelve tourism offices in Puerto López, while only two of the offices were locally owned. In more recent years the number of offices has increased, as have the number of outside investors. The end result is a situation in which local residents, including the members of PARCEMAR, have found it difficult to establish a presence in the growing tourism market.

In July 2003 the members of PARCEMAR organized a meeting to gain information about the appropriate course of action for obtaining financial assistance for their endeavor. I accompanied Manuel to Puerto López for the meeting on a rainy July afternoon. During the meeting, members of PARCEMAR took turns discussing the value of their tourism cooperative for local-level conservation as well as their desire to continue to grow. The primary goal of the meeting was to determine the amount of money required to meet PARCEMAR's needs. As the group discussed numbers and tried to figure out the income that would have to be generated to repay a loan of roughly US$10,000, Alfonso, the local development representative with whom the group was consulting, maintained that it would be difficult, if even feasible, to attain that amount. His T-shirt

FIGURE 5.1. *Sign promoting tourism in Salango*

extended a similar message in ironic fashion, stating "hay un mundo mejor, pero es carisimo" (there is a better world, but it is very expensive).

NGOs are still present throughout the region, but the successes of NGO-sponsored tourism projects have been minimal. NGO aid has been used primarily to promote tourism while not providing funds to develop the infrastructure needed for the transition from fishing and diving to tourism. Most notably, CISP used funds and labor to build signs promoting Salango as a tourist destination. The signs, which promote local tourist attractions including whale watching, Machalilla National Park, and the balsa festival (chapter 3) stand prominently along the highway that bisects the village. The signs make a tangential reference to the identity of the community with the phrase "Salango, 5,000 Years of History and Culture," a phrase that would be adopted in many of the community's efforts to promote tourism.

The signs present the casual observer with the image that development projects are being successfully negotiated in the rural communities of coastal Ecuador. However, the efforts of CISP to promote tourism in Salango occurred just prior to the scheduled end of the project cycle. NGO aid provided the means to attract tourists but did not sufficiently support the fundamental requirements of a cooperative, such as office space and reliable boat motors. The net result of CISP activity in Salango is that tourism offices are ill prepared to cater to tourists because of a lack of infrastructure.

Compounding the problems associated with a lack of government assistance and substantial NGO support was the disillusionment of members of PARCEMAR. In 2004 multiple members expressed an interest in selling their shares of the cooperative and running their own tours without its aid. Don Carlos, one of the founders and controlling members of the principal PARCEMAR office, reflected on the situation during a meeting in his makeshift office that I attended along with three members of the cooperative.

The office was a small space located in the front of his mechanic's shop and next to his home. The faded pastel walls were adorned with tourism posters and *Spondylus* shells, as well as a few ceramic artifacts that provided conversation pieces for tourists and a means of establishing a link to the past. Such adornments were common in tourism offices in Salango. Don Carlos entered his home for a moment and returned with multiple folders wrapped in plastic and filled with documents. One folder in particular contained a stack of yellow receipts. "It weighs a lot ... I cannot do this alone," he said referring to his belief that the cost of upkeep should not fall squarely on his shoulders. The frustration was clear on his face as he blamed the other members for not participating financially or physically. For their part, the others, some of whom were not present at the meeting out of protest, felt they had little to gain by participating since they did not have their own boats or motors, and in effect they believed they were being asked to finance something that would provide little benefit to them.

In the spring of 2005, two of the founding members sold their shares in favor of operating their own offices without the aid of the cooperative. In addition, Junior, a diver who appeared in a promotional video for Machalilla National Park, sold his share of the cooperative and decided to no longer pursue tourism. Sitting in his home, Junior maintained rather unequivocally, "One has to invest thousands of dollars ... for us that is very difficult ... tourism is very difficult. That is why I continue diving. I can make money by diving ... we can't live any other way." In the following years, PARCEMAR would no longer be a cooperative. The office and the original name were maintained by don Carlos, and he and his sons transitioned the cooperative into their own private tourism office and business. Despite these changes, tourism in Salango continued to grow, with opportunities and challenges presented in various forms.

CASE STUDY TWO: THE WORLD BANK AND COMMUNITY DEVELOPMENT

On a cool, damp afternoon in October 2007, I sat with don Angel in his humble home located in front of the beach. I have known don Angel for years. He is a short man with a thick build. Don Angel comes from a family of means, but he has little himself. When the weather is agreeable, he works his fields in la montaña. When the rains do not come, he makes a living from the ocean. In many ways he is the prototypical Salangueño. He is a child of Salango and has spent all of his sixty-plus years in the community in which he was born.

"It is lost money . . . it doesn't serve the people," he said as his face turned flush with anger. Don Angel was referring to the money the comuna had received for community-based tourism development projects—projects that according to many were ill-conceived and that have provided little benefit to the community as a whole.

Community development has long been a staple of the alternative development paradigm; consequently, it has a storied history, "waxing here, waning there, resurfacing or reasserting itself in different forms, places, and contexts" (Veltmeyer 2001:27). However, community-based tourism always involves the host community in planning, developing, and maintaining tourism projects (Blackstock 2005). As a form of "bottom-up" tourism, community-based tourism is founded on the premise that communities control tourism activities and that activities support local cultural forms while emphasizing sustainability (Ruiz-Ballesteros and Solis Carrión 2007). In addition, community-based tourism development ideally includes "equitable sharing of the control, division, and use of resources and of the ultimate benefits of development in a community" (Anacleti 2002:172). At its core, community-based tourism, or CBT as it is known by development practitioners, strives to engage local residents as active participants in development projects by affording communities control over organization and management of tourism operations (Ruiz-Ballesteros and Hernández Ramirez 2010). Even with such an apparently equitable approach to development, community-based development regularly fails to recognize how local practices mediate development processes.

One of the key issues at stake in development practices is the issue of power within the context of negotiating development. Development practices are inherently political; as such, scholars should attempt to understand and frame them as forms of political action (Ingamells 2007). It is within this context of understanding political dimensions of community development that I examine community-based tourism development.

The notion of "community" remains a point of contention for many anthropologists, and some view it with outright disdain because of its amorphous nature, the difficulty in defining exactly what constitutes community. Moreover, there is often a tendency to formulate an idealized notion of community. With reference to tourism and community, McIntyre, Hetherington, and Inskeep (1993:1) define community as "any homogenous place capable of tourism development . . . below the national and regional levels of planning." The mention of homogeneous is problematic. Challenges notwithstanding, I find it virtually impossible to avoid using the term *community* in the present discussion, and therefore I endeavor to continue forward while simultaneously recognizing the inherent deficiencies associated with such a term. These deficiencies include the fact that (1) the "concept of community serves to draw attention away from and ignore the internal class divisions and structural forces operating on individuals at this level" and instead presents an essentialized picture of economic, social, and political homogeneity (Veltmeyer 2001:27–28) that emphasizes unity and sameness over difference (Belsky 1999); (2) the concept of community frames community as a bound social entity when in reality communities overlap, intertwine, and intersect; and (3) the concept of community suggests a sense of permanence and immutability as opposed to recognizing that communities are constantly undergoing processes of change and transformation.

Even though the concept of community is riddled with complexities, borrowing from Gupta and Ferguson (2002:67), I conceptualize of community as consisting simultaneously of a physical space and "clusters of interaction" to which we can attribute certain ways of doing and a sense of social identity. It is from this point of departure that we can begin to gain a more nuanced understanding of community-based development.

Turismo comunitario (community-based tourism) was officially adopted in Ecuador in 2001, and in the spring of 2005, the comuna Salango made plans to begin a broad-based initiative to promote it. Prior to this time, most of the tourism development in Salango had occurred under the auspices of private development or, on some occasions, cooperative investment in tourism, such as the PARCEMAR case. The proposed community development plan was different from previous development efforts in that it was designed to initiate and develop turismo comunitario. The plan developed by the comuna outlines the following:

> In ten years the community of Salango will be a great center of tourism, ecology, fishing, agriculture, artisanship, culture, and science on the edge of the Ecuadorian coast, providing basic services that are harmoniously developed, planned, and sustainable; protecting, conserving the ecosystems and nature in general; making use of and administering appropriately its resources, cycles, and capacities; prepared to face and overcome threats with autonomy, organization, efficiency, participation, trust, solidarity, and transparency; working in complete

harmony and integration with the communities of Pueblo Manta; preserving its collective ancestral territory, its cultural and historical legacy, traditions; [and] exerting and respecting the rights corresponding to an ancestral community. (Plan Integral 2005)[2]

The development plan was produced in a time of community conflict, and it reflects this as it emphasizes not only economic development but also social and cultural development in the form of community "harmony" and "integration," as well as the need to "overcome threats" and develop a sense of "autonomy." All of these factors bear relation to the ongoing struggles elaborated in chapter 4.

While community development in Salango is specific to community politics and the tensions brought forth by struggles relating to the sale of communal lands, it is not independent of broader development considerations and in fact represents part of a global development apparatus. On July 5, 2001, the World Bank approved a loan to Ecuador in the amount of US$25.2 million. Funds for the loan were provided by the World Bank's International Bank for Reconstruction and Development and were secured by the Ecuadorian government in June 2002. The funds were part of a World Bank initiative known as PROLOCAL (Poverty Reduction and Rural Development Project), and monies were to be used for such varied activities as natural resource management, environmental protection, small business development, small-scale farming development, and sustainable tourism development (World Bank n.d.).

Keeping with the basic tenets of turismo comunitario, the comuna's plan consisted of multiple sub-projects, including fisheries development, environmental protection, and ecotourism and artisanal development. In the spring of 2006, funds were granted for three of the five projects outlined in the proposal. Surprisingly, funds were not granted for fisheries development or environmental protection. Instead, the sub-projects that received funds included Ecotourism and Community Development, Ecotourism and Artisanal Community Development, and Implementation of Integrated Farms in the Comuna Salango. A defining feature of each of the projects is a focus on local culture. This corresponds directly to the goals of turismo comunitario and represents one of the most promising aspects of CBT (Salazar 2012).

The sub-project Ecotourism and Community Development consisted of three related projects that focused on using the natural environment as a tourist attraction. The first phase of the sub-project was the planning and construction of a *sendero ecológico* (ecological hiking trail) in the inland montaña region. The second phase of the sub-project was the construction of a *mirador* (scenic overlook) on the crest of the southernmost point of the village of

FIGURE 5.2. *Construction of the mirador project*

Salango. The final phase of the project was the construction of a mirador in conjunction with the sendero ecológico.

The sub-project Ecotourism and Artisanal Community Development included the construction of a *taller artesanal* (artisans' workshop). The rationale for building the workshop was to give local artisans a place to work on their own crafts while also providing a space for younger generations to learn local craft traditions through formal classes. Ultimately, the construction of a community artisans' workshop would allow artisans to increase production and provide a more uniform line of products to the growing tourism market.

The sub-project Implementation of Integrated Farms in the Comuna Salango consisted of the construction of two *viveros* (plant nurseries) in the comuna Salango. One of the viveros was built in Río Chico and the other in Salango. The purpose of the viveros was to grow traditional plants such as citrus varieties, including oranges, limes, grapefruit, and others, as well as ornamental plants for communal use and for profit.

These three sub-projects form the core of the PROLOCAL-funded development efforts of the comuna. All of the projects were implemented in

FIGURE 5.3. *Inland vivero*

consultation with FEPTCE (*Plurinational Federation of Turismo Comunitario in Ecuador*) and CODENPE (Council for the Development of Nationalities and Peoples of Ecuador). The projects were executed between February and December 2006. In the pages that follow I place community-based development at the center of the struggle for political legitimacy. I pay close attention to local responses to and understanding of community-based development. The majority of the information presented in this section is drawn from my daily interactions with individuals involved in the projects. These individuals include, but are not limited to, comuna leaders, project *tecnícos* (technical experts), and various individuals who participated in the projects in some capacity. I also present data collected during follow-up interviews conducted in the fall of 2007.

Throughout Ecuador, the term *turismo comunitario* is used to describe tourism that is community-based inasmuch as the perceived benefits of tourism are not for the individual but for the community as a whole. Turismo comunitario differs from other types of tourism not only because it is "communal" in form but also because the dominant ideology behind it is one that attempts to provide tourists with an "authentic" experience of living in a rural Ecuadorian community. Tourists are encouraged to stay with local families and to take part in the practices of daily life to the extent to which they are comfortable. In this way turismo comunitario is meant to put the tourist face to face with local culture. The end result is a form of cultural tourism, sometimes also referred to as ethnic tourism. For Cole, cultural tourism is "motivated by the desire to experience a destination's culture" (Cole 2008:61). Ethnic tourism is conceived of in a slightly different way in that the emphasis is on marketing identity to the tourist (Wood 1984). In the case of turismo comunitario in Salango, local culture was being marketed to tourists. One brief example comes in the form of a hands-on workshop held for visiting university students at the artisans' workshop. The experience allowed the students to work with the *tagua* palm nut (*Phytelephas aequatorialis*) by carving it into jewelry. The same group also participated in workshops of traditional cooking and learned about the archaeology of the region through a tour and lecture at the museum.

A rhetoric of turismo comunitario permeates discussions of rural development strategies in Ecuador and serves as a cornerstone of rural development initiatives. The most significant proponents of turismo comunitario are the organizations CODENPE and FEPTCE. Each organization provides guidance and funding opportunities for development projects in Ecuador's Indigenous communities. The fact that CODENPE and FEPTCE provide oversight for development in Indigenous communities should not be overlooked and indeed is a significant detail that relates back to chapter 4 and Salango gaining status as an Indigenous/ancestral community. In obtaining such status, the community also achieved access to the institutional support of CODENPE and FEPTCE, which would ultimately prove necessary for the implementation of various community development projects. According to comuna vice president Ana Moran, a fundamental feature of projects supported by FEPTCE is that the "benefits do not go to the individual; benefits are for everyone, and FEPTCE helps to defend the rights of each community and support the projects of each community." This parallels FEPTCE's official position that situates tourism as a means to protect communal resources, including defending territory, while also promoting the visibility of alternative (native) cultural forms (FEPTCE 2007; Roux 2013). Thus, FEPTCE not only promotes development but also emphasizes community autonomy and decision-making as well as positioning itself to help support and protect communal resources and territories. All of these practices are reflected not only in turismo comunitario in Salango but also in the ongoing struggles related to identity and territory.

The casa comunal is a cavernous building with dim lighting and stale green paint on the walls. It is sparsely furnished and has been for as long as I can remember. In early February 2006 the building served as a cool oasis from the penetrating afternoon heat, and it was the location of a communal meeting regarding turismo comunitario. Prior to the meeting, most of the work regarding the projects existed only on paper. Thus, approximately fifty comuneros were in attendance to find out more about the proposed projects.

Roberto Toledo led the meeting and was assisted by the various tecnícos who were working with the comuna. Toledo spoke in an assured and measured tone. He exuded confidence and passion as he reported on the upcoming projects and the potential each of them held. One of the main objectives of the meeting was to provide tangible evidence that the projects were indeed soon to be under way. The corner of the building was filled with various items including plastic tubing, wheelbarrows, barbed wire, shovels, and other miscellaneous construction materials. The items were more than their material components. They represented the beginning of the projects and validated Toledo's authority and power as president of the comuna. Unlike previous comuna presidents, Toledo had made good on his promises. He was responsible for obtaining funds for the projects, and his success as a political leader was demonstrable by the supplies present at the meeting that day. Thus, the tangible markers of success gave credibility to Toledo's vision.

The success of the projects was paramount for Toledo's success as president of the comuna. Toledo took control of the comuna in 2004 under the precarious circumstances outlined in chapter 4, and he struggled to maintain support for his agenda. With this in mind, his focus on community development proved to be an avenue through which political legitimacy could be gained. Toledo's political aspirations were never a secret, and he was the target of substantial criticism during his time as comuna president. For those strongly opposed to Toledo, he was running a corrupt regime that benefited himself and his closest confidants both financially and politically. For Toledo's supporters, he was a revolutionary with strong moral principles and a willingness to fight for his community.

Toledo's success did not go unchallenged, despite his hard work and his focus on highlighting local culture through development. Community members voiced their discontent with the projects and Toledo. Some went so far as to suggest directly that community-based development in Salango was about nothing more than maintaining political control. Others accused Toledo of corruption and putting his political aspirations above the well-being of the community.

Turismo comunitario became a clear point of contestation shortly following the completion of projects in late 2006. Expectations were not met, and many community members were disenchanted. People expressed few misgivings about the projects themselves and instead were generally concerned about the lack of tangible results they generated. People who had previously supported the projects began to question their success, and tensions between the community's two factions were at an all-time high. By 2007 the projects had fallen into disrepair, and many residents criticized the projects and their ability to provide any monetary benefit to the community.

Questions about identity were not far removed from questions about the projects. Individuals who supported the development efforts also seemed to generally support the pro-Indigenous agenda to which the projects were attached. Critics of the comuna and of Toledo were quick to completely dismiss the notion of Indigenous identity. "We are mestizo, cholo, or montubio, but we are not Indian," asserted don Angel. In a radio interview conducted in late October 2007, the same message was broadcast to the listening public as the opposition brought identity to the table in a public display of discontent.

Other individuals made less direct comments about Indigenous identity, including Ana Moran, who maintained that while some members of the community did not embrace Indigenous identity, it was crucial to recognize the (pre) history of the region and establish a link to contemporary identity: "The history is important—if you ask someone here if they are Indigenous they say 'no,'—we need to recover the cultural identity of this place." Thus, the implementation of turismo comunitario was not only aimed at tourism development but was also in some manner a means of cultural revitalization by promoting Salango as a cultural and perhaps even an ethnic destination. However, not everyone in the community agreed with the projects or how they were being framed within the context of turismo comunitario and the newly realized Manta identity.

The tensions associated with turismo comunitario in Salango are symptomatic of the broader political tensions in the community and reflect an often existent gap between the "concept and implementation" of community-based development efforts (Stonich 2005:79). Critics of such efforts point to an all too frequent failure to recognize the heterogeneity of communities in favor of a tendency to view communities in idealized terms that emphasize homogeneity and harmony (Hernández Ramírez 2009; McLaren 1998; Stonich 2005). The case of turismo comunitario in Salango is reflective of this exact issue. Socioeconomic and political diversity along with political positioning pertaining to the land sale, some supporting and some against, created a challenging environment for the implementation of turismo comunitario.

Resident interpretations of turismo comunitario lend some clarity to the complexity of the situation while also pointing to the diversity of perspectives present in Salango. Many individuals were concerned that funds were not used in a manner that would benefit the majority of Salangueños: "The money was supposedly for turismo comunitario, but it stayed with the cabildo. They never took account of the general population . . . everything was done between eight to ten people . . . One percent [of the population] benefits, 99 percent didn't receive anything"; and "benefits for the community . . . there aren't many." When asked about participation in the projects, community members responded, "I didn't know anything about the projects," and "I did not participate first for a lack of communication . . . it appears to me that the group always works together. It is always only one group." These critiques point to a strong community sentiment that very few people were involved in the projects and therefore benefiting from them. Other community members shared generally positive views of turismo comunitario, stating, "It is something positive . . . not 100 percent but something positive," and "the community benefits . . . it is something good because they are doing many projects."

The implication here is that development does not exist outside the realm of local politics and local political agendas. Instead, just as development projects can be used to support the interests of national and international donor organizations, they can also be used as a mechanism for expanding and maintaining a local political base. In the case of turismo comunitario in Salango, it can be argued that tourism development shared a close camaraderie with political development. The implicit theme, then, is that development should be analyzed from a political perspective. Here I am referring to the underlying interests that help influence, facilitate, shape, and maintain development practices. It is not enough to merely look at relations of power and assume that grassroots or local economic development (LED) is somehow immune to the problems that are viewed as an inherent part of mainstream development.

CASE STUDY THREE: TOURISM AS A PRIVATE ENDEAVOR

Manuel, Diego, and I were at the speech given by presidential candidate Rafael Correa in Puerto López in October 2006. We had not intended to go to the speech. In fact, our visit to Puerto López was for a different reason, but the motive stands out in my mind now as related. We were there to catch a bus to Puerto Cayo for the purpose of buying a boat, as discussed earlier in this chapter. Both Manuel and Diego had dabbled in tourism prior to that time, and each was looking for a new means to generate income. In short, the decision to embark into the realm of tourism corresponded to a broader trend throughout the region and throughout Ecuador. Tourism was growing, and it was evident in Puerto López and other nearby towns and villages. Given the comuna's endeavor into turismo comunitario and an increasing interest in tourism by community members, it would just be a matter of time until tourism would be a prominent part of Salango's economy. Neither Diego nor Manuel was diving at the time; they had given up the occupation because of the restrictions in the Galapagos and the dangers and economic unpredictability of diving along the coast. Diego was working in the family restaurant, and Manuel toiled away working for his suegro don Jorge when needed. Occasionally, he would get don Jorge to lend him his fibra to make a run to the island with tourists, but it was anything but a formal endeavor. "There are lots of possibilities, tourism is growing," Manuel said to me on numerous occasions. The observation was true. Tourism in Salango was increasing little by little, and it appeared that more significant growth was eminent. There were already two tourism boats in Salango, and another two were being built. While working with the comuna and turismo comunitario was not a preferred choice, private tourism was.

We arrived in Puerto López to full streets and an air of excitement and anticipation that was not normal in the one stoplight town. It quickly became apparent that this was not an ordinary day. The crowd increased as we moved closer to the malecón and squeezed our way toward the front. The music of US hair band Twisted Sister's power anthem "We're Not Gonna Take It" blared over speakers stacked at the sides of the stage that was adorned with a large lime-green banner painted with the logo of Correa's political party, *Alianza País*. The song was a popular anthem of rebellion in the 1980s for angst-ridden youth who wanted to rise up against paternalism while rejecting conservative conventionality. The messages presented in the original English version translated well to Correa's campaign and his left-leaning political agenda that rejected US imperialism and promoted state autonomy and independence. Correa's campaign speech promoted his position that Ecuador needed to move away from a reliance on an oil-based economy, which tied the country to the United States and other consumers while at the same time creating a level of dependence. The solution Correa put forth was tourism.

After about ten minutes of listening to Correa's speech, Diego, Manuel, and I moved on to Puerto Cayo. A few weeks earlier los hermanos had negotiated to buy an old fishing fibra with the intent of fixing it up and converting it to a *lancha de turismo* (tourism boat). The fibra was rough around the edges and needed significant work. It would have to be widened and lengthened, and a top would have to be made for it. Constructing a small cabin would also be part of the process. Fortunately, don León was just the person for the job. Along with his skills as a master carpenter, don León was also the uncle of los hermanos, and he was willing to work for a reasonable price.

The ride back from Puerto Cayo was bumpy and winding. The three of us, along with the driver, crammed into the cab of the camión los hermanos had contracted to bring the fibra back to Salango. In a coincidence of sorts, the camión was adorned with a flag promoting Correa's campaign. It seemed as if all things were aligning; the decision to embark on a career in tourism was some-how validated by Correa's speech, and the flag on the camión only reinforced this validation. The choice to transport the fibra by land was made because of the long distance by ocean from Puerto Cayo to Salango and our lack of cer-tainty about the vessel's seaworthiness. Loading the fibra was a significant task. Fortunately, Diego and Manuel were able to get a group of sturdy-bodied men to help lift the hulking fiberglass vessel into the bed of the camión. This type of solicitation is common in the small communities of coastal Ecuador. I witnessed cases on numerous occasions where locals were willing to lend a helping hand, even to strangers, to aid in manual labor such as unloading sacks of cement or in this case loading a 9.5-meter-long fiberglass-hulled boat into the back of a truck. A small gift of US$20 would ensure a round of beers for them all.

The wooden sides of the truck groaned as the fibra was wedged into place. From the beach, the truck lurched toward the highway and the gears ground as the driver shifted with force to pick up speed. With each bump in the road, the fibra rose and fell with a massive thud that shook the entire camión. After about an hour we arrived in Salango. The truck lurched forward and then backed into place along the dirt street in front of the family home. Like most things in Salango that fall outside the ordinary routine, the unloading of the fibra was a bit of a spectacle as friends and neighbors arrived to look on and lend a helping hand.

I left Ecuador in late October, and in the months that followed don León worked with Diego and Manuel to rebuild the fibra. Don León usually worked building bongos or repairing small fibras, but he was also capable of working on larger boats. When he was not doing marine carpentry, he made doors for homes and cabinets and basically just about anything that could be built out of wood. Diego and Manuel sent me occasional photos of the progress on the fibra. After about six weeks of labor, the conversion was complete. Don León had transformed a rundown fishing fibra into a lancha ready for tourists.

Manuel and Diego arranged for their first tours in the early spring of 2007. They were extremely optimistic about what the future would hold. Part of their

FIGURE 5.4. *Unloading the fibra*

plan was to recruit tourists who visited the family restaurant and to make connections with various hostels, restaurants, and other businesses throughout the
area. Both Manuel and Diego viewed their foray into tourism as a means to
transform their lives. However, they were not free of struggles.

One of the major challenges encountered by Diego and Manuel, as well
as others working in tourism in Salango, was their ability to negotiate with
the national park and the local Ministry of Tourism office. The presence of
the national park increased corresponding to the growth of tourism, while
the park also played a role in enforcing restrictions related to tourism. Those
restrictions increased significantly under the Correa administration. In the
early days of tourism in Salango, guide licenses, captain licenses, and boat reg-
istrations were often overlooked; and there was a general understanding that
one could get around the requirements by paying a small bribe to a local official. The normalcy of such payments was made evident to me when a member
of the Ecuadorian Navy who was stationed in Puerto López came to Salango
to watch a voli match one afternoon. After the match, multiple boat operators
approached the *marino* and spoke with him for a few moments. At the end

Figure 5.5. *Lancha in front of Isla Salango*

of the conversation he was handed a few neatly folded bills. I later learned that the payment was an advance to overlook the boats when they went out with tourists the following day. What most in the United States would consider bribes were normal means of making things work in Ecuador, and little thought was given to such actions as moral or ethical compromises or "wrong." A little bit of money could easily help people avoid going through formal processes of paperwork and ease their ability to work in the informal economy that typified Ecuador. However, things would change.

"Hay muchos *trámites*" (there are lots of procedures), I was often told. The words came with a sense of frustration at the amount of work that had to be done to conduct tourism activities in a legal manner. The rhetoric of trámites was accompanied by a sense of unease about the changes taking place. The paperwork alone associated with the newly implemented trámites required a deep knowledge of legalese and some training. Business had not been conducted this way in the past. There were few, if any, documents to be signed, and in most cases one could work around the formal politics by calling on a friend or a compadre who had some leverage or knew somebody. In the worst cases, a small amount of money could be paid to make things happen. All of that was changing, and things were not as tranquilo as they once had been. As restrictions and trámites increased, so did the possibility of having one's boat impounded for not following the regulations set forth by the growing bureaucracy. This happened more than one time to El Gaucho, a local resident who switched from fishing to tourism but who did not follow all the guidelines put in place. His boat was taken to Puerto López and moored alongside the mobile navy station situated in the bay, a strong visual reminder to all of what would happen if the newly implemented regulations were not followed.

Not only did trámites become increasingly common, but the park also extended its reach by imposing regulations on boats from Salango. In particular, the park and the Ministry of Tourism advised Salango boat owners that they would no longer be able to leave from the local beach with tourists but instead would have to travel to Puerto López to pick up tourists. Although implemented prior to 2013, the change took full effect in that year with the inauguration of a new tourist pier in Puerto López. The opening of the pier, part of Correa's commitment to promote tourism along the Manabí coast, signified increasing challenges for operators from Salango. Most notably, tourist operators in Salango lamented the fact that they had to arrange tours from Puerto López. "It costs a lot, we have to go there and use fuel and then come back to go to the island . . . It doesn't make sense. It is a loss," related Diego. Behind his comments was the fact that he felt tourism favored Puerto López, in part because the offices of the park and the Ministry of Tourism are located there and in part because of the influence of wealthy investors in Puerto López. In addition, requiring boats to leave from Puerto López effectively eliminated operators' ability to take walkup tourists who visited one of the multiple offices in Salango. It also eliminated the ability of operators in Salango to recruit tourists who visited the local beach. For their part, tourists exhibited frustration and confusion at the fact that they could not just hire a local boat and leave from the beach. On numerous occasions the frustration resulted in tourists leaving Salango and going to Puerto López to hire a boat, only to find themselves back at the island a couple of hours later.

The trials encountered by resident tourism operators in Salango are the result of multiple factors. One of the most prominent is the presence of the national park and Ministry of Tourism offices in Puerto López. As a current operator stated, "The Ministry [of Tourism] does not exist in Salango." The lack of bureaucratic support resulted in operators in Salango feeling as though they were on the outside, on the periphery. In her detailed ethnography of development in East Africa, Walley (2004) suggests that bureaucracies can be sites of social struggle in which some groups are marginalized in favor of others, and the bureaucratic procedures associated with development practices often inhibit or limit access to participation. Tourism operators in Salango were acutely aware of this and often expressed their frustration that Puerto López as well as Agua Blanca, a small community located inland and within the boundaries of the national park, received preferential treatment from the Ministry of Tourism and park authorities.[3]

Despite the difficulties faced by Salango operators, changes in the form of access to technology and improvements to the highway are making tourism an increasingly important part of daily life in the village. Cell phone service arrived in 2005, and internet access is now present as well. Both of these means of communication support tourism, and operators are able to stay in close contact with tourists and others involved in tourism activities throughout the region. Announcements about tourism are now made on Facebook, and multiple operators have hundreds of followers and thousands of friends. Typical postings reference the "5,000 Years of History and Culture," and images promote the village's cultural offerings, including the balsa festival and the local museum. However, turismo comunitario remains largely separate from the private tourism offices in the community, mostly because of the complex politics associated with turismo comunitario and the comuna.

CONCLUSION: IDENTITY AND THE POLITICS OF DEVELOPMENT

Tourism development in Salango has taken various forms. Common to them all are two things: political dimensions and identity. With regard to identity, its relative importance lies along a continuum, with identity most prominent in the context of turismo comunitario. It is here that identity is closely aligned with local politics and the politics of state-level development organizations, including FEPTCE and CODENPE. Identity is far less embedded in the politics of development in the case of private endeavors into tourism or the cooperative project PARCEMAR. In both cases the political dimensions of identity are minimal. However, references to indigeneity and ancestrality are present as operators share stories with tourists about the past and display material markers of continuity, including *Spondylus* shells. Operators are also keen to make links to the region's prehistory as they take tourists on the water and describe how their ancestors, the Manteño, used to sail balsa rafts from Salango to various regions of the Pacific. There is also a practical continuity that creates a bridge between the labors of fishing and diving and tourism. Simply put, the operators of Salango acknowledge that they do what their ancestors did, inasmuch as they make a living from the Pacific Ocean. In essence, then, tourism practices reflect identity and belonging as conceived of by Salangueños.

While the case of cooperative and private efforts of tourism development points to challenges as well as opportunities, the case of turismo comunitario presents an appropriate context for examining the politics of development with reference to identity. It is no small fact that the growth of community-based tourism development in Salango corresponded directly to the rise of Indigenous politics in the village and surrounding area. Based on my experiences in coastal Ecuador during the rise of both locally fostered Indigenous politics and community-based tourism development, it became clear that the two processes were not mutually exclusive. The rhetoric in public and private discussions of development and Indigenous identity consistently blurred the boundaries between the two themes. In fact, it was often common for development to be couched in terms promoting "la identidad y historia del pueblo" (the identity and history of the village). This is a key component of FEPTCE's mission to advance turismo comunitario.

In a manner similar to Stronza's (2008) work on tourism development in the Peruvian Amazon and Trench's (2008) research in the Lacandón region of Mexico, in Salango identity was used to mediate development processes. As I have suggested, FEPTCE and CODENPE are prominent role players in Ecuadorian economic development and the politics of identity, as both organizations act as unifying bodies for the country's Indigenous pueblos. The significance of this dual position is that populations that are recognized as Indigenous have unique access to the support provided by FEPTCE and CODENPE. In Salango, the push for state recognition of Indigenous status in 2004 and the subsequent formation of Pueblo Manta in 2006 are representative of the politics of development. It was only through the self-articulation of Indigenous identity and the subsequent recognition of that identity that the was able to foster the relationships with FEPTCE and CODENPE that would ultimately result in the implementation of turismo comunitario in Salango.

Solidifying Salango's position as an Indigenous comunidad and a community that practices turismo comunitario was a legal shift of jurisdiction of the comuna from the Ministry of Agriculture to CODENPE. Moreover, the establishment and execution of the various turismo comunitario projects signified tangible representations of progress and change that justified Toledo's position of authority within the community. Thus, development in Salango was not solely about creating changes that benefit the community in social and economic terms. Development was a mechanism through which power was established, exerted, and maintained. As one local tourism operator expressed, "It is political . . . Here in Salango everything is political."

A final consideration is to explore the themes of continuity and change as they relate to tourism development in Salango. Tourism signifies change, but it is also relevant to reflect on continuity. Promoting tourism through a discourse of continuity by asserting a connection to the region's prehistory and the archaeological record is one component of tourism in Salango. This is seen in the adopted slogan "5,000 Years of History and Culture," as well as in the artifacts displayed in various tourism offices throughout the community. Even though a claim to continuity exists, continuity is more strongly asserted as tourism operators reflect on their own choice of livelihood and its connection to the storied history of the ocean-faring people of the Ecuadorian coast. We can thus think of this in the same terms addressed earlier in which economic practice is a cornerstone of continuity and fundamental to establishing a sense of belonging.

NOTES

1. Content from this chapter was previously published in *The Applied Anthropologist* (see Bauer 2007a).

2. En diez años la comunidad Salango será un gran centro turístico, ecológico, pesquero, agrícola, artesanal, cultural, y científico de la franja costa ecuatoriana, dotada de servicios básicos elementales, que se desarrolla armónica, planificada y sustentablemente; protegiendo, conservando los ecosistemas y la naturaleza en general; aprovechando y administrando de manera adecuada sus recursos, tiempos y capacidades, preparada para enfrentar y superar amenazas; con autonomía, organizada, eficiente, participativa, confiable, solidaria, y transparente; trabajando en plena armonía e integración con las comunidades de Pueblo Manta; preservando su territorio colectivo ancestral, su legado cultural e histórico, tradiciones; ejerciendo y respetando los derechos que como comunidad ancestral corresponden (Plan Integral, Comuna Salango, 2005, unpublished document).

3. Smith (2015) notes that being within the boundaries of Machalilla National Park creates a unique set of challenges for the community of Agua Blanca.

6

Closing

*Reflections on Change
and Continuity*

Every so often I review old photos I took in Salango and reflect on my time spent in the small ocean-side community. The earliest images are prints and the more recent are digital. When I find a particularly interesting image, I take a quick photo of it with my phone and send it to Diego or Manuel. The response is always a feeling of nostalgia and usually fondness. In a similar manner, Diego, Manuel, and I have spent lengthy periods of time looking through old photo albums they have in their homes. The albums, which rarely contain photos older than the early 2000s, point to a different life, and I am often reminded in conversations with local residents just how much things have changed in Salango within the last two decades. However, at the same time, there is a lasting continuity, a life made from the ocean and an archaeological record that stretches deep into the past but is present on a daily basis in the local museum and in the experience of encountering artifacts when partaking in mundane activities such as digging holes for construction or walking in the hills after the rain. These interactions shaped my own experiences in Salango and form the cornerstone of this book.

In the opening of this book I presented a brief reference to change by reflecting on an encounter at a local internet café. However, this book has been about much more than change caused by the introduction of new technologies such as the internet, cell phones, and similar developments. In fact, such transformations,

DOI: 10.5876/9781607327608.c006

while they might appear significant, are in no way as essential to understanding life in Salango as are the ongoing political and economic transformations that have shaped the community in recent decades. As such, I have focused only minimally on the visible markers of change and have instead emphasized the changes that are less conspicuous and that require a more nuanced insight into the local cultural and political context. From this, multiple themes have emerged under the general subject of continuity and change. These themes include, in no particular order, mestizaje, archaeology, identity, politics, and development.

Mestizaje is the fundamental ideology and form of identity politics present in Latin America, and it is a very real part of the experiences of the daily lives of many Ecuadorians. It is in response to mestizaje that Ecuador's Indigenous movements developed and gained force, particularly since the 1990s. Even though Ecuador's Indigenous movements have a pronounced history in the country's highland and Amazonian territories, recent mobilizations on Ecuador's coast continue to call into question the efficacy of mestizaje in both ideology and practice. However, movements on the coast, typified by the Manta-Wankavilka movement and addressed here with the Manta movement, present new questions about identity that are not characteristic of the highland and Amazonian contexts. In particular, the Manta movement asserts claims to an Indigenous identity in communities historically regarded as mestizo. Thus, challenging mestizaje was less about elevating or asserting rights pertaining to a previously existent Indigenous status and instead sought to stake claim to a formerly unrecognized identity. With this in mind, a question that emerges is, how or in response to what did such a transition in identity take place? Or perhaps a better question is, what was the catalyst for the emergence of the newly asserted identity? Following the work of Hill (1996) on ethnogenesis, I suggest that understanding Manta ethnogenesis requires an analysis of the cultural and political struggles that gave rise to the Manta identity while also paying attention to the historical consciousness of the people who make claim to that identity. Moreover, as I have suggested throughout this book, while the Manta identity is localized, it is imperative to recognize that it is connected to a broader national and global context.

In chapter 4 I use the metaphor of the road as a symbol of change while simultaneously reflecting on the very real way Ecuador's Highway E15 became a space for political struggle. I argue that the elaboration of E15 in the 1970s and again in the early 2000s influenced economic change in Salango while also connecting the village to outside agents of change, including NGOs and archaeologists. At the same time E15 became a conduit for transformation, control of the highway through a community paro in 2004 was a mechanism for asserting claims about identity.

The influence of outsiders in Salango extends to the growing political movement and land conflict that led to the assertion of an Indigenous identity. I posit that this can be understood in part by reflecting on the myth of the phantom. The phantom has always represented an outsider, and in its current manifestation it takes the form of a wealthy gringo who threatens the integrity of the community in much the same way as the phantom of lore. Responses to the land conflict can thus be viewed through the lens of history and local knowledge about conquest and colonization by the Spanish.

In the face of change, a perceived continuity to the past is referenced by Salangueños with regard to the archaeological record and material connections to *Spondylus*, as well as the permanency of economic practices used to make claims about identity. Such claims correspond to structural changes in the form of Ecuador's ratification of International Labour Organization (ILO) Convention 69 and the adoption of multiculturalism and, later, plurinationalism. With this in mind and corresponding to the work of French (2009), Anderson (2007), Brondo (2010), Latorre (2013), and Hooker (2005), I suggest that the emergence of the Manta identity is not only a response to the dominant ideology of mestizaje but is the result of the creation of a legal framework that allows for and even facilitates the assertion of non-mestizo ethnic identities. Moreover, I propose that while significant changes have occurred in Salango with claims made to an Indigenous/ancestral identity and the assertion of Manta identity, I also argue that identity is used as a means for negotiating development through formal connections to powerful agents of change, including the Council for the Development of Nationalities and Peoples of Ecuador (CODENPE) and the Plurinational Federation of Turismo Comunitario in Ecuador (FEPTCE). It is through a discourse of continuity that transformations, including claims to identity and development, take place.

The case studies presented in chapter 5 illustrate the varied and complex forms of tourism development practices in Salango. Similar to the politics of identity, the political dimensions of tourism development in Salango are subject to influences that extend well beyond the village boundaries. Turismo comunitario, as adopted by the comuna Salango, represents a state-sponsored attempt to promote tourism while also linking village-level practices to international funding agencies and national support structures, including the World Bank, CODENPE, and FEPTCE, in much the same way Indigenous politics in Salango link up with the Confederation of Indigenous Nationalities of

Ecuador (CONAIE). While turismo comunitario is part of a state-sponsored project, it is heavily subject to local political practices and institutions. Most notably, the ongoing process of staking claim to an Indigenous/ancestral identity proved to be a means for securing access to development resources that simultaneously legitimized local-level political agendas. Just as turismo comunitario represents a prominent part of tourism development, so do cooperative and private tourism ventures. While an emphasis on identity is not an explicit component of either, in the same way it is central to understanding turismo comunitario, tourism is viewed as a continuation of the economic relationship with the Pacific Ocean that has defined Salango for millennia.

One of the things I do not address explicitly in this book is the question of authenticity. This is a conscious decision I made for multiple reasons. I chose not to focus on authenticity because I find it problematic for myself as an outsider to question the authenticities of experiences and identities associated with residents of rural coastal Ecuador. Doing so would represent a continuation of the paternalism associated with the history of colonialism and mestizaje in Latin America. Related to this, I recognize that multiple "authentic" experiences can exist; as such, we should not be concerned with validating authenticity but instead with examining the ways claims to identity, perhaps framed as authenticity, are negotiated (Lucero 2006). I have attempted to employ this approach while being careful not to engage in an elaborate discussion of the authenticity of local expressions of and claims to identity. A second reason for not delving into a discussion of authenticity is the fact that claims to Manta identity are aligned with parameters for self-identification associated with ILO Convention 169. Authenticity is not part of the criteria outlined in the convention. Instead, the focus is on claims to territory and cultural practices. It is through ritualized cultural practices such as the balsa festival, knowledge of the archaeological record, and the everyday interactions associated with a livelihood reliant on the Pacific Ocean that Salangueños stake claim to their identity.

Identity and belonging emerge as prominent themes of this study. Most notably, the data presented in chapter 4 on resident self-identification illustrate the complex ways community members conceive of their own position in Ecuadorian society and their sense of self. This is informed by the dominant paradigm of mestizaje and reflects components of Salangueño historical consciousness. I approach identity and belonging as complementary elements of self, whether conceived of individually or collectively. Identity is expressed as a means of establishing and maintaining difference. Identity, as expressed by the adoption of the Manta identity, is also deeply political; corresponding to Cervone (1998), the case of Salango provides a context for investigating how ethnic identity can be converted into a political instrument. In contrast, belonging is associated with asserting a sense of sameness or a quality of likeness. For Salangueños, belonging is associated with a profound connection to community and an attachment to place that is nurtured through shared experiences that are in no small part related to the economic aspects of life in a small ocean-side village.

A final consideration is to acknowledge the changing scope of ethnic politics and identity in Ecuador and how such changes are negotiated at the local level and experienced as part of the lived reality of rural Ecuadorians. The central paradox associated with this is how claims to continuity are a mechanism for change. It was only through the establishment of a connection to the past and the archaeological record that Salangueños were able to stake claim to and gain recognition as an Indigenous community while simultaneously gaining access to support for tourism development.

In closing, the case study presented in this book points to the dynamic nature of identity as well as complex and varying perspectives on identity and belonging and continuity and change. Even in the face of significant changes, Salangueños retain a deep connection to the past and its relation to the present. While Salango's past extends back 5,000 years, it is always present just below the surface of the community.

Fieldwork for this book took place between 2002 and 2014. I returned to Salango in December 2016 after a two-year absence and completion of the writing of the initial draft of this book. Returning to Salango was like returning to a familiar home where physical changes had occurred, including changes to the local museum and expansion of the local park and soccer field/outdoor auditorium, but where family, relationships, and the pace of daily life remain much the same. Community politics, tourism, development, and identity were topics that remained at the surface of my conversations with locals.

On a warm evening just before Christmas, I sat with Manuel and his wife, María, at the dining table in their home. The space was once the apartment I had built on the side of Manuel's house after the theft I experienced at the museum. In the years following my dissertation research and my less frequent visits to Salango, Manuel transformed the apartment to expand his own living space for his growing family. In addition, he surprised me with a separate apartment, built with money he saved working for the national park. He hoped to rent the apartment to tourists and travelers and to reserve it for me when I was in Ecuador. For Manuel, tourism is the future of Salango. His ideas had changed little from my first encounters with him as a member of PARCEMAR in 2002. His life, however, had changed dramatically. He had gone from living in a small room in his parents' home with his wife and

DOI: 10.5876/9781607327608.c007

first child while scraping out a living working early mornings on his suegro's fibra to constructing and expanding his own home, opening his tourism business with Diego, and, later, gaining a government job with a secure salary. It is only now as I write this that I think back to how much Manuel's life has changed in the last fifteen years. To me, it is an impressive story that is beyond the scope of this book but that might find itself in the pages of my future writings.

Manuel, María, and I engaged in a conversation that was similar in form but not theme to numerous conversations we had had over the course of more than a decade. The routine was familiar, and despite two years away from Salango, it was as though things had changed but time had not. This was something I frequently experienced when returning to visit a village and people who had such a significant impact on my life, not only professionally but also personally. Manuel, María, their children, and I had become family despite our extraordinarily different backgrounds and experiences. We shared countless meals and conversations over the course of my fieldwork, and the dialogue that took place in December 2016 represented another chapter in after-dinner talks that bridged more than a decade and that tended to focus on community events and politics. It was an update of sorts, but more than anything I came away from the conversation with a sense that while great political strides had been made, few tangible benefits had been gained from the community-based development efforts.

In the years since the bulk of my research ended, Manuel took a job with the national park and subsequently terminated his working relationship with Diego. Manuel was still working in tourism, but he found himself on a different side of things. Even so, he, like most residents of Salango, maintained an interest in local politics and continued to view tourism as important for the community's future. For her part, María always maintained a quiet demeanor and only rarely voiced a strong opinion. She always struck me as the type of person who gave a great deal of thought to her words before she spoke. If Manuel was strong and sometimes boisterous, María was his complement—small in stature and voice but thoughtful and analytical.

"They are beginning new projects," María said with a slight tone of aggravation. She was referring to the comuna. "Yes, they are building the mirador . . . you know how much [it will cost]?" interjected Manuel. "Thirteen thousand dollars." "*Rebuilding* the mirador, right?" I inquired. "Yes, the same one."

And so the conversation continued, reflecting on the projects that had been completed nearly a decade prior and the comuna's continued push to secure funds for community development efforts. In some cases projects were new; in other cases funds were being requested to redo projects that were part of the World Bank initiative. In all cases the focus was turismo comunitario; although the efforts emphasized the comunidad or pueblo in name, they were still centered around the political institution of the comuna.

As a result of Manuel's increasing commitment to his work for the national park, Diego purchased Manuel's share of their struggling tourism company. This played out in numerous phone calls to me from both Diego and Manuel during my absence from the field. I served as a bit of a sounding board at times when the brothers had trouble communicating with one another because of their differing opinions. They both expressed the challenges of working together and of generating an income for two growing families while relying on an unpredictable and increasingly competitive foray into tourism. In the end, it made sense for them to part ways. Maintaining their relationship as brothers was more important than maintaining a business relationship.

During that same visit in late 2016, Diego informed me that many of the original members of PARCEMAR had reunited in an effort to collaborate with the national park to gain management rights over a small and fairly isolated beach located just north of the village. Shortly after the rights were granted, Diego shared a short promotional video produced by the national newspaper *El Universo*. Diego and don Carlos, both original members of PARCEMAR, appear in the video and serve as guides for the publicity that aims to promote Salango as a tourism destination. While the video and the recognition of Salango in national media are significant, what stood out for me was one element. Only moments into the video, don Carlos notes a large tree along the trail that leads to the beach. He pauses briefly in a moment of reflection and explains the tree's significance. He makes note of its use as the material for constructing the balsa rafts navigated by the Manteño, whom he refers to as "*nuestros antepasados*" (our ancestors). It was just another example of how the past is seemingly always present in the daily lives of locals.

My visit to Salango in December 2016 reinforced much of what I have tried to present in this book. I found myself back in a community that, while maintaining a deep connection to the past, faces challenges as the political and economic landscape of the region changes. However, residents are not passive recipients of change. They are instead active and conscientious agents who think critically about their own identities and the future of Salango while being acutely aware of the ability of the past to shape the future.

aguaje. Uncharacteristically strong waves and current.

ahijado. Ritual kin term used to refer to one's godson.

al pulmón. Diving done without compressed air. Literally, "by the lung."

albacora. Highly valued type of tuna.

Alianza País. Ecuadorian political party founded by Rafael Correa in 2006.

alzamiento indígena. Literally, "Indigenous revolt." The term was used to refer to the 1990 Indigenous uprising (see Whitten and Whitten 2011).

apodo. Nickname. The practice of referring to people by nicknames is common in Ecuador.

arroz con pollo. Chicken with rice. A typical dish on the Ecuadorian coast.

bajo. Fishing site characterized by an increased depth relative to the surrounding ocean floor.

balsas. Wooden rafts.

Barbudazo. Descriptive term used to describe someone who is heavily bearded.

barcos. Literally, "boats." Used to refer to large fishing boats.

barcos pesqueros. Literally, "fishing boats." Used to refer to large fishing boats.

blanqueamiento. Process of cultural "whitening" described by Whitten (2003b), Whitten and Fine (1981), and Whitten and Quiroga (1998).

bolones. Balls made of either fried or boiled plantains. A food that is very typical in coastal Ecuador.

bongos. Small wooden rowboats.

bonito. Type of small tuna common in Ecuadorian coastal waters.

cabaña. Literally, "cabin."

cabildo. Directors' council of the comuna.

camioneta. Pickup truck.

caña. Local firewater made from sugarcane; also, bamboo.

cantina. Small bar; often a corner store that also serves alcohol.

cantón. Municipal capital.

capitán. Captain of a boat or ship.

carretera. Highway.

casa comunal. Community center where offices of the directorship are located and community meetings are held.

CEDESA (Centro Juvenil del Desarrollo de Salango). Youth Center for the Development of Salango.

chinchorreros. Large wooden fishing boats.

cholo. Individual of mixed descent, most often Indigenous and Spanish. The term can carry derogatory connotations of ignorant and low status but can also be used as a term of endearment for close friends and family.

CIMS. Centro de Investigaciones Museo Salango.

claro. The lunar period including the full moon and the few days preceding the full moon. Used to indicate the time when the moon is brightest.

CODENPE (Consejo de Desarrollo de las Nacionalidades y Pueblos del Ecuador). Council for the Development of Nationalities and Peoples of Ecuador. A government organization that focuses specifically on development in Indigenous communities.

comadre. Ritual kin term used to refer to the mother of one's godchild, or used by parents to refer to the godmother of their own child.

comerciantes. Term used to refer to traders who buy and sell fish and seafood, most often purchasing directly from fishermen and selling to local restaurants.

compa. Colloquial term used to refer to one's compadre, or co-father.

compadrazgo. Set of social relationships that binds individuals as a result of godparenthood.

compadre. Ritual kin term used to refer to the father of one's godchild. The term is also used in-kind by the child's parents to refer to the male godparent.

compañeros. Literally, "companions." Often used in political speech to refer to political supporters or those who are on the same "team."

comuna. Minimal unit of governmental oversight in Ecuador, consisting of one or more villages or hamlets that share common access to land. The comuna is responsible for the administration and allocation of communal lands.

comuneros. Registered members of the comuna.

CONAIE (Confederación de Nacionalidades Indígenas del Ecuador). Confederation of Indigenous Nationalities of Ecuador. Ecuador's national Indigenous organization.

CONFENAIE (Confederación de Nacionalidades Indígenas de la Amazonia del Ecuador). Confederation of Indigenous Nationalities of the Ecuadorian Amazon.

corviche. Typical coastal Ecuadorian dish consisting of fish or shrimp encased in plantain dough and deep-fried.

corvina. Type of sea trout common in coastal Ecuadorian waters. Often referred to as "sea bass."

costa. Literally, "coast." Used to refer to Ecuador's coastal region.

cumbia. Type of dance music that has Caribbean origins but is common throughout Latin America.

don. Term of honor or respect used to refer to a man who is held in high regard. The term can also be used as a marker of status, with people of lower social position adopting it to refer to a man of higher social position.

doña. Term of honor or respect used to refer to a woman who is held in high regard. The term can also be used as a marker of status, with people of lower social position adopting it to refer to a woman of higher social position.

ECUARUNARI (Confederación de los Pueblos Indígenas Kichwas del Ecuador). Confederation of Indigenous Kichwa Peoples of Ecuador. Regional organization associated with the Ecuadorian highlands.

El Día de la Raza. Literally, "Day of the Race." Celebrated throughout Latin America every October 12 to pay homage to the Latin American who is the product of European, African, and Indigenous influences.

El Festival de la Balsa Manteña. Celebration of Indigenous heritage in Salango and surrounding communities. Occurs each October 12 and was first celebrated in 1992.

El Suizo. Term used to refer to the Swiss investor.

El Universo. National newspaper published in Guayaquil.

encomendero. Grantees of encomienda lands.

encomienda. System of land tenure in which grantees were allotted control of both land and Indigenous inhabitants, who were expected to pay tribute.

Estatuto del Pueblo Manta. Literally, "Statute of Pueblo Manta." Document containing the founding principles of Pueblo Manta.

fantasma. Literally, "phantom."

FEPTCE (Federación Plurinacional del Turismo Comunitario del Ecuador). Plurinational Federation of Turismo Comunitario in Ecuador. Government organization that promotes and oversees community-based tourism for Ecuador's various nationalities.

fibras. Small fiberglass fishing boats with outboard motors.

fiesta. Literally, "party."

fritadas. Ecuadorian dish consisting of fried pork pieces.

Fundación Pro Pueblo. International NGO that is prominent throughout Ecuador and that managed Museo Salango from 1995 to 2005.

Fundación Presley Norton. Foundation that managed Museo Salango from 1987 to 1995.

fútbol. Literally, "football" (soccer).

gancho. Literally, "hook." Used to refer to the large metal hooks often used in fishing.

garua. Light rain that comes down as a mist and is most typical in the months of May through August in the Salango region.

gasolinera. Gas station.

gaveta. Plastic bin used for transporting goods. Also a unit of measure applied to fish and other seafood products.

gaveteros. Individuals who work transporting full gavetas from boats to trucks.

gringo. Term used throughout Ecuador to refer to a foreigner from the United States but also used more generally to refer to a foreigner who is phenotypically "white."

guato. Prized gamefish known in English as a "Goliath Grouper."

hacienda. Large landed estate.

hijos del pueblo. Literally, "children of the village."

huacas. Locations of ritual significance believed to be inhabited by gods or spirits.

huasipungo. System of debt peonage associated with the Ecuadorian highlands.

La República de los Indios. Literally, "the Republic of Indians." Formal division of Spanish-controlled colonial Latin America that recognized Indians as a separate legal group from Spaniards.

la Señorita Manteña Bonita. Beauty pageant associated with Salango's balsa festival.

lancha de turismo. Tourism boat or yacht.

langosta. Lobster.

levantamiento indígena. Indigenous uprising. Differs from alzamiento indígena in that it does not carry the same negative connotations but instead implies rising up or standing up for one's rights.

Ley de Organización y Régimen de Comunas (Ley de Comunas). Law enacted in 1937 that allows for the formation of a comuna as the minimal political unit in Ecuador.

los hermanos. Literally, "the brothers."

machismo. Emphasis on masculinity in Latin American culture.

malecón. Boardwalk.

Manteño. Culture that inhabited the south-central Ecuadorian coast from approximately AD 800 until the Spanish conquest in the 1500s.

marino. Sailor.

mestizaje. Latin American ideology of ethno-racial mixing that privileges European over Indigenous cultural markers.

mestizo/a. Person of mixed European (Spanish) and Indigenous descent.

mezclados. Literally, "mixed." Used by locals to refer to "mixed" ethnic heritage.

mi pana. Term of endearment that indicates friendship. Akin to "my friend" in English.

Ministerio de Agricultura. Ministry of Agriculture.

MIPMAWPU (El Movimiento Indígena de los Pueblos Manta Wankavilkas y Punaés). Indigenous Movement of Manta Wankavilka and Punaé Peoples.

mirador. Scenic lookout.

montaña. Literally, "mountain." Used by coastal residents to refer to the inland region that is defined by increased elevation in the form of low-lying hills.

montubio. Coastal-dwelling peasant of mixed descent (often Spanish, Indigenous, and African).

municipio. Municipality. Also used to refer to the municipal headquarters (building).

negra. Species of small tuna that is common in the waters off the Ecuadorian coast.

oriente. Literally, "the Orient" or "the East." Used in Ecuador to refer to the Amazonian territory on the eastern edge of the country.

oscuro(s). Period of the lunar cycle when moonlight is limited, approximately twenty-five days of the month. Considered by locals to be the best time for fishing.

otro hermano. Literally, "another brother."

pacha mama. Kichwa term referring to "Mother Earth."

Pachakutik Nuevo País. Political arm of CONAIE.

padrino. Literally, "godfather."

parcela marina. Literally, "marine plot." The term refers to a protected area off the coast of Salango.

PARCEMAR. Tourism cooperative that helped establish Salango's parcela marina.

paro. Strike or protest.

parroquia. The minimal administrative unit that connects communities to the state government.

patrones. Patrons or bosses.

peones. Laborers or peons.

pepino. Sea cucumber.

Pilsener. Ecuador's national beer.

pishtaco. Andean bogeyman who preys on Indigenous men and women.

pomas. Large plastic containers ranging in size from approximately three to ten gallons used to transport fuel.

PROLOCAL (Poverty Reduction and Rural Development Project). World Bank–funded project that allocated over $25 million to Ecuador for rural development.

provincia. Literally, "province."

Pueblo Manta. Political entity and ethnic designation consisting of the comunas of Salango, Agua Blanca, Las Tunas, and El Pital.

Pueblo Manta-Huancavilca. Political entity and ethnic designation consisting of numerous comunas throughout Manabí, Santa Elena, and Guayas provinces.

quintal(es). Unit of measure. One "quintal" is equal to 100 pounds.

raíces ancestrales. Literally, "ancestral roots."

rasgos indígenas. Indigenous racial features.

red. Fishing net. The term is most commonly used to refer to large seine nets.

reducciones. Settlements of Indians associated with missions during the colonial period.

sala. Living room.

salud. Literally, "health." Salutation given when drinking. Akin to "cheers" in the English language.

sendero ecológico. Ecological hiking trail. Built as part of the turismo comunitaria efforts in Salango.

sierra. Term used to refer to Ecuador's highland Andean region.

sucre. Official currency of Ecuador from 1884 to 2000.

suegro. Father-in-law.

tagua. Palm nut common to tropical regions of coastal Ecuador. Frequently referred to as vegetable ivory.

taller artesanal. Literally, "artisans' workshop."

tecnícos. Trained experts or technicians.

terrenos ancestrales. Literally, "ancestral lands."

terrenos comunales. Literally, "communal lands," lands controlled and administered by the comuna.

tienda. Small store.

trámites. Literally, "procedures" or "proceedings." Often used to refer to things that are a hassle.

tranquilo. Literally, "tranquil" or "peaceful."

turismo comunitario. Community-based tourism.

un aguita. General term used for a tea or herbal remedy made from medicinal plants that has curative properties.

un duro. Someone who is powerful or who has influence.

unas tostadas. Toasted bread.

Valdivia. Phase of occupation of coastal Ecuador that dated from approximately 3100 to 1400 BC.

vivero(s). Plant nurseries.

voli. Popular Ecuadorian sport related to volleyball but with slightly different rules.

Abbot, Thomas. 2013. "Oil Drilling in Ecuador's Yasuní National Park: Correa's Drive towards Development at Any Price." Council on Hemispheric Affairs. Accessed September 12, 2014. http://www.coha.org/oil-drilling-in -ecuadors-yasuni-national-park-correas-drive-towards -development-at-any-price/.

Aberle, David. 1987. "Distinguished Lecture: What Kind of Science Is Anthropology?" *American Anthropologist*, New Series 89 (3): 551–66.

Álvarez, Silvia. 1999. *De Huancavilcas a Comuneros: Relaciones Interétnicas en la Península de Santa Elena, Ecuador.* Quito: Abya-Yala.

Anacleti, Odhiambo. 2002. "Research into Local Culture: Implications for Participatory Development." In *Development and Culture*, ed. Deborah Eade, 168–73. London: Oxfam Great Britain.

Anderson, Benedict. 1983. *Imagined Communities: Reflections on the Origin and Spread of Nationalism.* London: Verso.

Anderson, Mark. 2007. "When Afro Becomes (Like) Indigenous: Garifuna and Afro-Indigenous Politics in Honduras." *Journal of Latin American and Caribbean Anthropology* 12 (2): 384–413. https://doi.org/10.1525/jlat.2007.12.2.384.

Anthias, Floya. 2008. "Thinking through the Lens of Translocational Positionality: An Intersectionality for Understanding Identity and Belonging." *Translocations: Migration and Social Change* 4 (1): 5–20.

Arguedas, José María. 2002. *Los Ríos Profundos.* Trans. Frances Horning Barraclough. Prospect Heights, IL: Waveland.

DOI: 10.5876/9781607327608.c008

Banks, Marcus. 1996. *Ethnicity: Anthropological Constructions*. London: Routledge. https://doi.org/10.4324/9780203417935.

Baquero, Andrés. 2002. *El Parque Nacional Machalilla: Un Parque en Peligro*. Quito: Fundación Natura and the Nature Conservancy.

Barkin, David. 2001. "Neoliberalism and Sustainable Popular Development." In *Transcending Neoliberalism: Community-Based Development in Latin America*, ed. Henry Veltmeyer and Anthony O'Malley, 184–204. Bloomfield, CT: Kumarian.

Barth, Fredrik. 1998. "Introduction." In *Ethnic Groups and Boundaries: The Social Organization of Cultural Difference*, ed. Fredrik Barth, 9–38. Prospect Heights, IL: Waveland.

Bauer, Daniel. 2007a. "Negotiating Development: Local Actors and Economic Change in Coastal Ecuador." *The Applied Anthropologist* 27 (2): 118–28.

Bauer, Daniel. 2007b. "The Reinvention of Tradition: An Ethnographic Study of *Spondylus* Use in Coastal Ecuador." *Journal of Anthropological Research* 63 (1): 33–50. https://doi.org/10.3998/jar.0521004.0063.104.

Bauer, Daniel. 2008. "Negotiating Development: Identity and Economic Practice in Coastal Ecuador." PhD dissertation, Southern Illinois University, Carbondale.

Bauer, Daniel. 2010a. "Re-articulating Identity: The Shifting Landscape of Indigenous Politics and Power on the Ecuadorian Coast." *Bulletin of Latin American Research* 29 (2): 170–86. https://doi.org/10.1111/j.1470-9856.2009.00347.x.

Bauer, Daniel. 2010b. "Tradición e Identidad Cultural." *Revista de Antropología Experimental* 10 (1): 183–94.

Bauer, Daniel. 2012. "Emergent Identity, Cultural Heritage, and El Mestizaje: Notes from the Ecuadorian Coast." *Journal of Latin American Cultural Studies* 21 (1): 103–21. https://doi.org/10.1080/13569325.2011.652601.

Bauer, Daniel. 2014. "Becoming Manta: Archaeology, Place, and Meanings of Indigeneity." *Ethnology* 50 (4): 319–31.

Bauer, Daniel, and Richard Lunniss. 2010. "The Past in the Present: *Spondylus*, Place, and Identity." *Latin Americanist* 54 (3): 75–94. https://doi.org/10.1111/j.1557-203X.2010.01077.x.

Bazurco Osorio, Martín. 2006. *"Yo Soy Más Indio Que Tú" Resignificando la Etnicidad: Exploración Teórica e Introducción al Proceso de Reconstrucción Étnica en las Comunas de la Península de Santa Elena, Ecuador*. Quito: Abya-Yala.

Bebbington, Anthony. 1992. "Grassroots Perspectives on 'Indigenous' Agricultural Development: Indian Organizations and NGOs in the Central Andes of Ecuador." *European Journal of Development Research* 4 (2): 132–67. https://doi.org/10.1080/09578819208426574.

Bebbington, Anthony. 1997. "Social Capital and Rural Intensification: Local Organizations and Islands of Sustainability in the Rural Andes." *Geographical Journal* 163 (2): 189–97. https://doi.org/10.2307/3060182.

Beck, Scott, and Kenneth J. Mijeski. 2011. *Pachakutik and the Rise and Decline of the Ecuadorian Indigenous Movement*. Athens: Ohio University Press.

Becker, Marc. 1997. "Class and Ethnicity in the Cantón of Cayambe: The Roots of Ecuador's Modern Indian Movement." PhD dissertation, University of Kansas, Lawrence.

Becker, Marc. 1999. "Comunas and Indigenous Protest in Cayambe Ecuador." *Americas* 55 (4): 531–59. https://doi.org/10.2307/1008320.

Becker, Marc. 2008. *Indians and Leftists in the Making of Ecuador's Modern Indigenous Movements*. Durham, NC: Duke University Press. https://doi.org/10.1215/9780 822381457.

Becker, Marc. 2010. "The Children of 1990." *Alternatives* 35 (3): 291–316. https://doi .org/10.1177/030437541003500307.

Belsky, Jill M. 1999. "Misrepresenting Communities: The Politics of Community-Based Rural Ecotourism in Gales Point Manatee, Belize." *Rural Sociology* 64 (4): 641–66. https://doi.org/10.1111/j.1549-0831.1999.tb00382.x.

Benavides, O. Hugo. 2008. "Archaeology, Globalization, and the Nation: Appropriating the Past in Ecuador." In *Handbook of South American Archaeology*, ed. Helaine Silverman and William Isbell, 1063–72. New York: Springer. https://doi.org/10 .1007/978-0-387-74907-5_53.

Benavides, O. Hugo. 2011. "Indigenous Representations of the Archaeological Record: Spectral Reflections of Postmodernity in Ecuador." In *Indigenous Peoples and Archaeology in Latin America*, ed. Cristóbal Gnecco and Patricia Ayala, 251–68. Walnut Creek, CA: Left Coast.

Binns, Tony, and Etienne Nel. 1999. "Beyond the Development Impasse: The Role of Local Economic Development and Community Self-Reliance in Rural South Africa." *Journal of Modern African Studies* 37 (3): 389–408. https://doi.org/10.1017 /S0022278X99003067.

Biord, Horacio. 2006. "Dinámicas étnicas y demarcación de territorios indígenas en el Nororiente de Venezuela." *Antropológica* 105–6: 131–60.

Blackstock, Kirsty. 2005. "A Critical Look at Community Based Tourism." *Community Development Journal: An International Forum* 40 (1): 39–49. https://doi.org /10.1093/cdj/bsi005.

Blower, David. 1995. "The Quest for Mullu: Concepts, Trade, and the Archaeological Distribution of Spondylus in the Andes." MA thesis, Trent University, Peterborough, ON.

Borah, Woodrow. 1954. "Race and Class in Mexico." *Pacific Historical Review* 23 (4): 331–42. https://doi.org/10.2307/3634652.

Bretón Solo de Zaldívar, Victor. 2002. "Cooperación al Desarrollo, Capital Social y Neo-Indigenismo en los Andes Ecuatorianos." *Revista Europea de Estudios Latinoamericanos y del Caribe* 73: 43–63.

Briones, Claudia. 2003. "Re-membering the Dis-membered: A Drama about Mapuche and Anthropological Cultural Production in Three Scenes." *Journal of Latin American Anthropology* 8 (3): 31–58. https://doi.org/10.1525/jlca.2003.8.3.31.

Brondo, Keri Vacanti. 2010. "When Mestizo Becomes (Like) Indio . . . or Is It Garifuna? Negotiating Indigeneity and 'Making Place' on Honduras' North Coast." *Journal of Latin American and Caribbean Anthropology* 15 (1): 171–94. https://doi .org/10.1111/j.1935-4940.2009.01058.x.

Buckley, Ralf. 2010. *Conservation Tourism.* Wallingford: CAB International. https://doi.org/10.1079/9781845936655.0000.

Canessa, Andrew. 2006. "Todos somos indígenas: Towards a New Language of National Political Identity." *Bulletin of Latin American Research* 25 (2): 241–63. https://doi.org/10.1111/j.0261-3050.2006.00162.x.

Carter, Benjamin, and Matthew Helmer. 2015. "Elite Dress and Regional Identity: Chimú-Inka Perforated Ornaments from Samanco, Nepeña Valley, Coastal Peru." *BEADS: Journal of the Society of Bead Researchers* 27: 46–74.

Cervone, Emma. 1998. "Los Desafíos de la Etnicidad: Las Luchas del Movimiento Indígena en la Modernidad." *Journal of Latin American Anthropology* 4 (1): 46–73. https://doi.org/10.1525/jlca.1998.4.1.46.

Cervone, Emma. 2012. *Long Live Atahualpa: Indigenous Politics, Justice, and Democracy in the Northern Andes.* Durham, NC: Duke University Press. https://doi.org/10 .1215/9780822395096.

Clifford, James. 1986. "Introduction." In *Writing Culture: The Poetics and Politics of Ethnography,* ed. James Clifford and George E. Marcus, 1–26. Berkeley: University of California Press.

Cohen, Abner. 1969. *Custom and Politics in Urban Africa: A Study of Hausa Migrants in Yoruba Towns.* London: Routledge and Kegan Paul.

Cohen, Percy. 1969. "Theories of Myth." *Man* 4 (3): 337–53. https://doi.org/10.2307/2 798111.

Cole, Stroma. 2008. *Tourism, Culture, and Development: Hopes, Dreams, and Realities in Eastern Indonesia.* Clevedon, UK: Channel View.

Colloredo-Mansfeld, Rudi. 2002. "Autonomy and Interdependence in Native Movements: Towards a Pragmatic Politics in the Ecuadorian Andes." *Identities (Yverdon)* 9 (2): 173–95. https://doi.org/10.1080/10702890212205.

Colloredo-Mansfeld, Rudi. 2009. *Fighting Like a Community: Andean Civil Society in an Era of Indian Uprisings.* Chicago: University of Chicago Press. https://doi.org /10.7208/chicago/9780226113876.001.0001.

Confederación de Nacionalidades Indígenas del Ecuador. 2007. "Propuesta de la CONAIE frente a la Asamblea Constituyente: Principios y lineamientos para la nueva constitución del Ecuador, Por un Estado Plurinacional, Unitario, Soberano, Incluyente, Equitativo y Laico." Quito: Confederatión de Nacionalidades Indígenas del Ecuador. Accessed January 15, 2014. http://www.iee.org.ec/publicaciones /INDIGENA/ConaieAsamblea.pdf.

Confederación de Nacionalidades Indígenas del Ecuador (CONAIE). n.d. "Pueblos y Nacionalidades." Accessed January 23, 2014. https://www.conaie.org/nacional idades-y-pueblos.

Conklin, Beth A. 1997. "Body Paint, Feathers, and VCRs: Aesthetics and Authenticity in Amazonian Activism." *American Ethnologist* 24 (4): 711–37. https://doi.org /10.1525/ae.1997.24.4.711.

Constitución Política de la República del Ecuador. 1998. Political Database of the Americas. Georgetown University, Washington, DC. Accessed January 5, 2014. http://pdba.georgetown.edu/Constitutions/Ecuador/ecuador98.html.

Constitución Política de la República del Ecuador. 2008. Political Database of the Americas. Georgetown University, Washington, DC. Accessed January 5, 2014. http://pdba.georgetown.edu/Constitutions/Ecuador/english08.html.

Cruz Rodríguez, Edwin. 2012. "Redefiniendo la Nación: Luchas Indígenas y Estado Plurinacional en Ecuador (1990–2008)." *Nómadas: Revista Critica de Ciencias Sociales y Jurídicas*, vol. Especial: América Latina: 469–91.

Currie, Elizabeth J. 1995. "Archaeology, Ethnohistory, and Exchange along the Coast of Ecuador." *Antiquity* 69 (264): 511–26. https://doi.org/10.1017/S0003598X000 81904.

Díaz-Andreu, Margarita, and Timothy Champion, eds. 2015. *Nationalism and Archaeology in Europe*. New York: Routledge.

Escobar, Arturo. 1995. *Encountering Development: The Making and Unmaking of the Third World*. Princeton, NJ: Princeton University Press.

Esteva-Fabregat, Claudio. 1994. *Mestizaje in Ibero-America*. Trans. John Wheat. Tucson: University of Arizona Press.

Faiola, Anthony. 2008. "Calling Foreign Debt 'Immoral,' Leader Allows Ecuador to Default." *Washington Post*, December 13. Accessed March 28, 2018. http://www.was hingtonpost.com/wp-dyn/content/article/2008/12/12/AR2008121204105.html.

Federación Plurinacional del Turismo Comunitario del Ecuador. 2007. *Guía del Turismo Comunitario del Ecuador*. Quito: Federación Plurinacional del Turismo Comunitario del Ecuador.

French, Jan Hoffman. 2004. "Mestizaje and Law Making in Indigenous Identity Formation in Northeast Brazil: 'After the Conflict Came the History.'" *American Anthropologist* 106 (4): 663–74. https://doi.org/10.1525/aa.2004.106.4.663.

French, Jan Hoffman. 2009. *Legalizing Identities: Becoming Black or Indian in Brazil's Northeast.* Chapel Hill: University of North Carolina Press. https://doi.org/10.5149/9780807889886_french.

Friedman, Jonathan. 1992. "The Past in the Future: History and the Politics of Identity." *American Anthropologist* 94 (4): 837–59. https://doi.org/10.1525/aa.1992.94.4.02a00040.

Gaibor, Nikita, Javier Rosero, and Manfred Altamirano. 2002. *El Impacto de La Migración Humana en Las Artes de Pesca Artesenales y Semi-Industriales Utilizadas en Los Parques Nacionales Galápagos (Isla Isabela) y Machalilla.* Quito: Fudación Natura and the Nature Conservancy.

García, María Elena, and José Antonio Lucero. 2011. "Authenticating Indians and Movements: Interrogating Indigenous Authenticity, Social Movements, and Fieldwork in Contemporary Peru." In *Histories of Race and Racism: The Andes and Mesoamerica from Colonial Times to the Present,* ed. Laura Gotkowitz, 278–98. Durham, NC: Duke University Press. https://doi.org/10.1215/9780822394334-013.

García Canclini, Néstor. 1993. *Transforming Modernity: Popular Culture in Mexico.* Trans. Lidia Lozano. Austin: University of Texas Press.

Gaytán, Marie Sarita. 2008. "From Sombreros to *Sincronizadas*: Authenticity, Ethnicity, and the Mexican Restaurant Industry." *Journal of Contemporary Ethnography* 37 (3): 314–41. https://doi.org/10.1177/0891241607309621.

Gobierno del Ecuador. n.d. Resultados del Censo 2010. Accessed January 23, 2014. http://www.ecuadorencifras.gob.ec/resultados/.

Gonzales, Tirso, and Miguel González. 2015. "Introduction: Indigenous Peoples and Autonomy in Latin America." *Latin American and Caribbean Ethnic Studies* 10 (1): 1–9. https://doi.org/10.1080/17442222.2015.1034437.

Gordon, Edmund T., and Charles R. Hale. 2003. "Rights, Resources, and the Social Memory of Struggle: Reflections and Black Community Land Rights on Nicaragua's Atlantic Coast." *Human Organization* 62 (4): 369–81. https://doi.org/10.17730/humo.62.4.7ca3booqhkv955t2.

Graber, Yann, and Nicole Jastremski. 2009. "Étude d'une tombe collective de l'époque Manteño (Salango, Equateur) dans son contexte, culturel et funéraire, regional." *Antropo* 18: 9–25.

Gudeman, Stephen. 2001. *The Anthropology of Economy: Community, Market, and Culture.* Malden, MA: Blackwell.

Gupta, Akhil, and James Ferguson. 2002. "Beyond 'Culture': Space, Identity, and the Politics of Difference." In *The Anthropology of Globalization: A Reader,* ed. Jonathan Xavier Inda and Renato Rosaldo, 65–80. Malden, MA: Blackwell.

Gutiérrez Chong, Natividad. 2010. "Indigenous Political Organizations and the Nation-State: Bolivia, Ecuador, Mexico." *Alternatives* 35 (3): 259–68. https://doi.org/10.1177/030437541003500305.

Hale, Charles. 1997. "The Cultural Politics of Identity in Latin America." *Annual Review of Anthropology* 26 (1): 567–90. https://doi.org/10.1146/annurev.anthro.26.1.567.

Hall, Stuart. 1990. "Cultural Identity and Diaspora." In *Identity: Community, Culture, Difference*, ed. Jonathan Rutherford, 222–37. London: Lawrence and Wishart Limited.

Handler, Richard. 1986. "Authenticity." *Anthropology Today* 2 (1): 2–4. https://doi.org/10.2307/3032899.

Harris, Michael, Valentina Martínez, William J. Kennedy, Charles Robert, and James Gammack-Clark. 2004. "The Complex Interplay of Culture and Nature in Coastal South-Central Ecuador." *Expedition* 46 (1): 38–43.

Herlihy, Laura Hobson. 2012. *The Mermaid and the Lobster Diver: Gender, Sexuality, and Money on the Miskito Coast*. Albuquerque: University of New Mexico Press.

Hernández Ramírez, Macarena. 2009. "Adentrándonos en la ruta del spondylus: comienzos del Turismo Comunitario en la Comunidad de Salango." In *Cultura, Comunidad, y Turismo: Ensayos sobre el Turismo Comunitario en Ecuador*, ed. Esteban Ruiz Ballesteros and María Augusta Vintimilla, 383–433. Quito: Abya Yala.

Hernández Ramírez, Macarena, and Esteban Ruiz Ballesteros. 2011. "Etnogénesis como Práctica: Arqueología y Turismo en el Pueblo Manta (Ecuador)." *Revista de Antropología Iberoamericana* 6 (2): 159–92. https://doi.org/10.11156/aibr.060203.

Hill, Jonathan D. 1996. "Introduction: Ethnogenesis in the Americas, 1492–1992." In *History, Power, and Identity: Ethnogenesis in the Americas, 1492–1992*, ed. Jonathan D. Hill, 1–19. Iowa City: University of Iowa Press.

Hill, Jonathan D., and Thomas M. Wilson. 2003. "Identity Politics and the Politics of Identities." *Identities (Yverdon)* 10 (1): 1–8. https://doi.org/10.1080/10702890304336.

Hooker, Juliet. 2005. "Indigenous Inclusion/Black Exclusion: Race, Ethnicity, and Multicultural Citizenship in Latin America." *Journal of Latin American Studies* 37 (2): 285–310. https://doi.org/10.1017/S0022216X05009016.

Ibarra, Alicia. 1996. "Los Indios del Ecuador y Su Demanda Frente al Estado." In *Democracia y Estado Multiétnico en América Latina*, ed. Pablo Casanova González and Marcos Roitman Rosenman, 293–320. Mexico City: Centro de Investigaciones Interdisciplinarias en Ciencias y Humanidades; UNAM; La Jornada Ediciones.

Ingamells, Ann. 2007. "Community Development and Community Renewal: Tracing the Workings of Power." *Community Development Journal: An International Forum* 42 (2): 237–50. https://doi.org/10.1093/cdj/bsi111.

International Labour Organization. 1989. "C169—Indigenous and Tribal Peoples Convention, 1989 (no. 169)." Accessed January 5, 2014. http://www.ilo.org/dyn/normlex/en/f?p=NORMLEXPUB:12100:0::NO:12100:P12100_ILO_CODE:C169.

Jokisch, Brad, and Jason Pribilsky. 2002. "The Panic to Leave: Economic Crisis and the 'New Emigration' from Ecuador." *International Migration* 40 (4): 75–102. https://doi.org/10.1111/1468-2435.00206.

Kistler, S. Ashley. 2014. *Maya Market Women: Power and Tradition in San Juan Chamelco, Guatemala*. Urbana: University of Illinois Press.

Kohl, Philip L., and Clare Faucett, eds. 1995. *Nationalism, Politics, and the Practice of Archaeology*. Cambridge: Cambridge University Press.

Latorre, Sara. 2013. "The Politics of Identification in a Shrimp Conflict in Ecuador: The Political Subject, 'Pueblos Ancestrales del Ecosistema Manglar' [Ancestral Peoples of the Mangrove Ecosystem]." *Journal of Latin American and Caribbean Anthropology* 18 (1): 67–89. https://doi.org/10.1111/jlca.12003.

León, Jorge. 1994. *De Campesinos a Cuidadanos Diferentes: El Levantamiento Indígena*. Quito: CEDIME—Abya Yala.

Lucero, José Antonio. 2003. "Locating the 'Indian Problem': Community, Nationality, and Contradiction in Ecuadorian Indigenous Politics." *Latin American Perspectives* 30 (1): 23–48. https://doi.org/10.1177/0094582X02239143.

Lucero, José Antonio. 2006. "Representing 'Real Indians': The Challenges of Indigenous Authenticity and Strategic Constructivism in Ecuador and Bolivia." *Latin American Research Review* 41 (2): 31–56. https://doi.org/10.1353/lar.2006.0026.

Lunniss, Richard. 2001. "Archaeology at Salango, Ecuador: An Engoroy Ceremonial Site on the South Coast of Manabí." PhD dissertation, University of London, London, UK.

Lunniss, Richard. 2008. "Where the Land and the Ocean Meet: The Engoroy Phase Ceremonial Site at Salango, Ecuador, 600–100 BC." In *Pre-Columbian Landscapes of Creation and Origin*, ed. John Edward Staller, 203–48. New York: Springer. https://doi.org/10.1007/978-0-387-76910-3_7.

Macas, Luís. 2007. "Abusos Contra el Pueblo Manta-Wankavilca en Salango." *Boletín de Prensa*, July 30. Press release, Confederatión de Nacionalidades Indígenas del Ecuador, Quito.

Marcos, Jorge. 1986. "Breve Prehistoria del Ecuador." In *Arqueología de la Costa Ecuatoriana: Nuevos Enfoques*, ed. Jorge Marcos, 25–50. Quito: Corporación Editora Nacional.

Martin, Alexander J. 2001. "The Dynamics of Precolumbian Spondylus Trade across the South American Central Pacific Coast." MA thesis, Florida Atlantic University, Boca Raton.

Martin, Alexander J. 2007. "El Intercambio de Spondylus a lo largo de la costa sudamerica, de acuerdo al registro arqueológico." In *II Congreso Ecuatoriano de Antropología y Arqueología*, Tomo I: *Balance de la última década: Aportes, Retos y nuevos temas*, ed. Fernando García, 433–62. Quito: ABYA-YALA y Banco Mundial Ecuador.

Martin, Alexander J. 2009. "The Domestic Mode of Production and the Development of Sociopolitical Complexity: Evidence from the Spondylus Industry of Ecuador." PhD dissertation, University of Pittsburgh, Pittsburgh, PA.

Martínez, Valentina. 1997. "Excavaciónes en el Sitio Arquelógico Río Chico Provincia Sur de Manabí: Escuela de Campo de Arqueológica." Unpublished professional report. Guayaquil: Escuela Superior Politécnica Littoral.

Martínez, Valentina, Yann Graber, and Michael Harris. 2006. "Estudios Interdisciplinarios en la Costa Centro-Sur de la Provincía de Manabí (Ecuador): Nuevos Enfoques." *Boletín del Instituto Francés de Estudios Andinos* 35 (3): 433–44. https://doi.org/10.4000/bifea.3956.

Martínez Novo, Carmen. 2006. *Who Defines Indigenous: Identities, Development, Intellectuals, and the State in Northern Mexico.* New Brunswick, NJ: Rutgers University Press.

Martínez Novo, Carmen. 2014. "The Minimization of Indigenous Numbers and the Fragmentation of Civil Society in the 2010 Census in Ecuador." *Journal of Iberian and Latin American Research* 20 (3): 399–422. https://doi.org/10.1080/13260219.2014 .995877.

Masucci, Maria A. 1995. "Marine Shell Bead Production and the Role of Domestic Craft Activities in the Economy of the Guangala Phase, Southwest Ecuador." *Latin American Antiquity* 6 (1): 70–84. https://doi.org/10.2307/971601.

McEwan, Colin. 2003. "And the Sun Sits in His Seat: Creating Social Order in Andean Culture." PhD dissertation, University of Illinois, Urbana-Champaign.

McEwan, Colin, María Isabel Silva, and Chris Hudson. 2006. "Using the Past to Forge the Future: The Genesis of the Community Site Museum at Agua Blanca, Ecuador." In *Archaeological Site Museums in Latin America*, ed. Helaine Silverman, 187–216. Gainesville: University of Florida Press.

McIntyre, George, Arlene Hetherington, and Edward Inskeep. 1993. *Sustainable Tourism Development: Guide for Local Planners.* Madrid: World Tourism Organization.

McLaren, Deborah. 1998. *Rethinking Tourism and Ecotravel: The Paving of Paradise and What You Can Do to Stop It.* Sterling, VA: Kumarian.

Meggers, Betty J. 1966. *Ecuador.* London: Thames and Hudson.

Ministerio de Turismo. n.d.a. Accessed June 12, 2016. http://servicios.turismo.gob.ec /index.php/anuario-de-estadisticas-turisticas.

Ministerio de Turismo. n.d.b. Accessed June 12, 2016. http://servicios.turismo.gob.ec /index.php/anuario-de-estadisticas-turisticas.

Morales Cano, Lucero, and Avis Mysyk. 2004. "Cultural Tourism, the State, and Day of the Dead." *Annals of Tourism Research* 31 (4): 879–98. https://doi.org/10.1016/j .annals.2004.03.003.

Moreno Parra, Héctor Alonso, and Alejandra Machado Maturana. 2011. "Group-Differentiated Rights and the Multicultural State in Colombia." In *Multiculturalism in the Americas: Canada and the Americas*, ed. Patrick Imbert, 71–104. Ottawa: University of Ottawa.

Murra, John V. 1963. "The Historic Tribes of Ecuador." In *Handbook of South American Indians*, vol. 2: *The Andean Civilizations*, ed. Julian Steward, 785–821. New York: Cooper Square.

Narotzky, Susana. 1997. *New Directions in Economic Anthropology*. London: Pluto.

Norton, Presley. 1986. "El Señorío de Salangome y la Liga de Mercaderes: El Cartel Spondylus-Balsa." Boletín de los Museos del Banco Central del Ecuador. *Miscelánea Antropológica Ecuatoriana* 6: 131–44.

Norton, Presley, Richard Lunniss, and Nigel Nayling. 1983. "Excavaciones en Salango, Provincia de Manabí, Ecuador." *Miscelánea Antropológica Ecuatoriana* 3 (3): 9–72.

Osborne, Brian S. 2006. "From Native Pines to Diasporic Geese: Placing Culture, Setting Our Sites, Locating Identity in a Transnational Canada." *Canadian Journal of Communication* 31 (1): 147–75. https://doi.org/10.22230/cjc.2006v31n1a1781.

Pallares, Amalia. 2002. *From Peasant Struggles to Indian Resistance: The Ecuadorian Andes in the Late Twentieth Century*. Norman: University of Oklahoma Press.

Paulsen, Allison C. 1974. "The Thorny Oyster and the Voice of God: Spondylus and Strombus in Andean Prehistory." *American Antiquity* 39 (4): 597–607. https://doi.org/10.2307/278907.

Pierotti, Raymond. 2011. *Indigenous Knowledge, Ecology, and Evolutionary Biology*. New York: Routledge.

Plan Integral, Comuna Salado. 2005. Unpublished document.

Pribilsky, Jason. 2007. *La Chulla Vida: Gender, Migration, and the Family in Andean Ecuador and New York City*. Syracuse, NY: Syracuse University Press.

Pueblo Manta. 2005. "Estatuto Pueblo Manta." Unpublished document.

Radcliffe, Sarah. 1990. "Marking the Boundaries between the Community, the State, and History in the Andes." *Journal of Latin American Studies* 22 (3): 575–94. https://doi.org/10.1017/S0022216X00020964.

Radcliffe, Sarah. 2000. "Entangling Resistance, Ethnicity, Gender, and Nation in Ecuador." In *Entanglements of Power: Geographies of Domination/Resistance*, ed. Joanne P. Sharpe, Paul Routledge, Chris Philo, and Ronan Paddison, 164–81. London: Routledge.

Reck, Gregory. 1986. *In the Shadow of Tlaloc: Life in a Mexican Village*. Prospect Heights, IL: Waveland.

Roitman, Karem. 2008. "Hybridity, Mestizaje, and Montubios in Ecuador." QEH Working Paper Series. Working Paper no. 165, 1–19.

Roitman, Karem. 2009. *Race, Ethnicity, and Power in Ecuador: The Manipulation of Mestizaje*. London: First Forum.

Rostworowski, Maria, and Craig Morris. 1999. "The Fourfold Domain: Inka Power and Its Social Foundations." In *The Cambridge History of the Native Peoples of the Americas*, vol. 3: *South America, Part 1*, ed. Frank Salomon and Stuart B. Schwartz, 769–863. Cambridge: Cambridge University Press. https://doi.org/10.1017/CHOL 9780521630757.012.

Roux, Fanny. 2013. *Turismo Comunitario Ecuatoriano, Conservación Ambiental y Defensa de los Territorios*. Quito: Federación Plurinacional del Turismo Comunitario del Ecuador.

Rowe, Sarah. 2012. "Mestizo, Nativo, Indígena: Archaeology and Authenticity in the Creation of Ecuadorian Coastal Indigenous Identities." Paper presented at the 30th International Congress of the Latin American Studies Association, San Francisco, CA, May 23–26.

Ruiz-Ballesteros, Esteban, and Doris Solis Carrión. 2007. *Turismo Comunitario en Ecuador: Desarrollo y sostenibilidad social*. Quito: Abya-Yala.

Ruiz-Ballesteros, Esteban, and Macárena Hernández-Ramírez. 2010. "Tourism That Empowers? Commodification and Appropriation in Ecuador's *Turismo Comunitario*." *Critique of Anthropology* 30 (2): 201–29. https://doi.org/10.1177/0308275X 09345426.

Ruiz Navas, José Mario. 2013. "Son solo indios." *El Universo*. Accessed January 13, 2014. eluniverso.com.

Sahlins, Marshall. 1972. *Stone Age Economics*. New York: Aldine de Gruyter.

Salazar, Noel B. 2012. "Community-Based Cultural Tourism: Issues, Threats, and Opportunities." *Journal of Sustainable Tourism* 20 (1): 9–22. https://doi.org/10.1080 /09669582.2011.596279.

Salomon, Frank, and George L. Urioste. 1991. *The Huarochirí Manuscript: A Testament of Ancient and Colonial Andean Religion*. Austin: University of Texas Press.

Sandstrom, Alan R. 2008. "Blood Sacrifice, Curing, and Ethnic Identity among Contemporary Nahua of Northern Veracruz, Mexico." In *Ethnic Identity in Nahua Mesoamerica: The View from Archaeology, Art History, Ethnohistory, and Contemporary Ethnography*, ed. Frances F. Berdan, John K. Chance, Alan R. Sandstrom, Barbara L. Stark, James M. Taggart, and Emily Umberger, 150–82. Salt Lake City: University of Utah Press.

Sandweiss, Daniel. 1999. "The Return of the Native Symbol: Peru Picks *Spondylus* to Represent New Integration with Ecuador." *Society for American Archaeology Bulletin* 17 (2): 8–9.

Sawyer, Suzana. 2004. *Crude Chronicles: Indigenous Politics, Multinational Oil, and Neoliberalism in Ecuador*. Durham, NC: Duke University Press. https://doi.org/10.1215/9780822385752.

Segarra, Monique. 1997. *Embedding Political Identity: Professionalizing NGOs in Ecuador*. Papers on Latin America. New York: Columbia University Institute of Latin American Studies.

Selverston-Scher, Melina. 2001. *Ethnopolitics in Ecuador: Indigenous Rights and the Strengthening of Democracy*. Miami: North-South Press Center.

Shepherd, S. A., P. Martinez, M. V. Toral Granda, and G. J. Edgar. 2004. "The Galápagos Sea Cucumber Fishery: Management Improves as Stocks Decline." *Environmental Conservation* 31 (2): 102–10. https://doi.org/10.1017/S0376892903001188.

Shimada, Izumi. 1999. "Evolution of Andean Diversity: Regional Formations (500 BCE–CE 600)." In *The Cambridge History of the Native Peoples of the Americas*, vol. 3: *South America, Part 1*, ed. Frank Salomon and Stuart B. Schwartz, 350–517. Cambridge: Cambridge University Press. https://doi.org/10.1017/CHOL9780521630757.007.

Silverman, Helaine, ed. 2006. *Archaeological Site Museums in Latin America*. Gainesville: University Press of Florida.

Smith, Kimbra. 2015. *Practically Invisible: Coastal Ecuador, Tourism, and the Politics of Authenticity*. Nashville, TN: Vanderbilt University Press.

Solimano, Andrés. 2002. "Crisis, Dollarization, and Social Impact: An Overview." In *Crisis and Dollarization in Ecuador: Stability, Growth, and Social Equity*, ed. Paul Beckerman and Andrés Solimano, 1–16. Washington, DC: World Bank.

Southon, Michael. 1985. "Sea Tenure and Modernization on the Central Coast of Ecuador." BA thesis, Australian National University, Canberra.

Stark, Barbara L., and John K. Chance. 2008. "Diachronic and Multidisciplinary Perspectives on Mesoamerican Ethnicity." In *Ethnic Identity in Nahua Mesoamerica: The View from Archaeology, Art History, Ethnohistory, and Contemporary Ethnography*, ed. Frances F. Berdan, John K. Chance, Alan R. Sandstrom, Barbara L. Stark, James M. Taggart, and Emily Umberger, 1–37. Salt Lake City: University of Utah Press.

Stephen, Lynn. 1996. "The Creation and Re-creation of Ethnicity: Lessons from the Zapotec and Mixtec of Oaxaca." *Latin American Perspectives* 23 (2): 17–37. https://doi.org/10.1177/0094582X9602300202.

Stonich, Susan C. 2005. "Enhancing Community-Based Tourism Development and Conservation in the Western Caribbean." *NAPA Bulletin* 23 (1): 77–86. https://doi.org/10.1525/napa.2005.23.1.77.

Stronza, Amanda. 2008. "Through a New Mirror: Reflections on Tourism and Identity in the Amazon." *Human Organization* 67 (3): 244–57. https://doi.org/10.17730/humo.67.3.a556044720353823.

Stutzman, Ronald. 1981. "*El Mestizaje*: An All-Inclusive Ideology of Exclusion." In *Cultural Transformations and Ethnicity in Modern Ecuador*, ed. Norman E. Whitten Jr., 45–94. Urbana: University of Illinois Press.

Sunkel, Osvaldo. 2005. "The Unbearable Lightness of Neoliberalism." In *Rethinking Development in Latin America*, ed. Charles H. Wood and Bryan R. Roberts, 55–78. University Park: Pennsylvania State University Press.

Thomas, Nicholas. 1992. "The Inversion of Tradition." *American Ethnologist* 19 (2): 213–32. https://doi.org/10.1525/ae.1992.19.2.02a00020.

Tilley, Virginia Q. 2005. "*Mestizaje* and the 'Ethnicization' of Race in Latin America." In *Race and Nation: Ethnic Systems in the Modern World*, ed. Paul Spickard, 53–68. New York: Routledge.

Treasury Reporting Rates of Exchange as of March 31, 1988. Department of the Treasury, Financial Management Service. Accessed March 23, 2018. https://www.gpo.gov/fdsys/pkg/GOVPUB-T63_100-e1f3dbccf36c1e9c8762b7d3cabd6cb5/pdf/GOVPUB-T63_100-e1f3dbccf36c1e9c8762b7d3cabd6cb5.pdf.

Treasury Reporting Rates of Exchange as of March 31, 2000. Department of the Treasury, Financial Management Service. Accessed March 23, 2018. https://www.gpo.gov/fdsys/pkg/GOVPUB-T63_100-961cf6145650a813eb61a4d466e3aa2b/pdf/GOVPUB-T63_100-961cf6145650a813eb61a4d466e3aa2b.pdf.

Trench, Tim. 2008. "From 'Orphans of the State' to the *Comunidad Conservacionista Institucional*: The Case of the Lacandón Community, Chiapas." *Identities (Yverdon)* 15 (5): 607–34. https://doi.org/10.1080/10702890802333827.

Tsing, Anna Lowenhaupt. 2001. "Nature in the Making." In *New Directions in Anthropology and the Environment: Intersections*, ed. Carole L. Crumley, A. Elizabeth van Deventer, and Joseph J. Fletcher, 3–23. Walnut Creek, CA: Altamira.

Van Cott, Donna Lee. 2005. *From Movements to Parties in Latin America*. Cambridge: Cambridge University Press. https://doi.org/10.1017/CBO9780511756115.

Vasconcelos, José. 1925. *La Raza Cósmica, Misión de la Raza Iberoamericana*. Paris: Agencia Mundial de Librería.

Veltmeyer, Henry. 2001. "The Quest for Another Development." In *Transcending Neoliberalism: Community-Based Development in Latin America*, ed. Henry Veltmeyer and Anthony O'Malley, 1–34. Bloomfield, CT: Kumarian.

Villamarín, Juan, and Judith Villamarín. 1999. "Chiefdoms: The Prevalence and Persistence of 'Señoríos Naturales,' 1400 to European Conquest." In *The Cambridge History of the Native Peoples of the Americas*, vol. 3: *South America, Part 1*, ed. Frank Salomon and Stuart B. Schwartz, 577–667. Cambridge: Cambridge University Press. https://doi.org/10.1017/CHOL9780521630757.009.

Wade, Peter. 1997. *Race and Ethnicity in Latin America*. Sterling, VA: Pluto.

Walley, Christine J. 2004. *Rough Waters: Nature and Development in an Eastern African Marine Park.* Princeton, NJ: Princeton University Press. https://doi.org /10.1515/9781400835751.

Warren, Kay B. 1998. *Indigenous Movements and Their Critics: Pan-Maya Activism in Guatemala.* Princeton, NJ: Princeton University Press.

Warren, Kay B., and Jean E. Jackson. 2002. "Introduction: Studying Indigenous Activism in Latin America." In *Indigenous Movements, Self-Representations, and the State in Latin America,* ed. Kay B. Warren and Jean E. Jackson, 1–46. Austin: University of Texas Press. https://doi.org/10.4324/9780203215432_chapter_1.

Weismantel, Mary. 2000. "Race Rape: White Masculinity in Andean Pishtaco Tales." *Identities (Yverdon)* 7 (3): 407–40. https://doi.org/10.1080/1070289X.2000.9962673.

Weismantel, Mary. 2003. "Mothers of the *Patria*: La Chola Cuencana and La Mama Negra." In *Millennial Ecuador: Critical Essays on Cultural Transformations and Social Dynamics,* ed. Norman E. Whitten Jr., 325–54. Iowa City: University of Iowa Press.

Whitten, Norman E., Jr. 1965. *Class, Kinship, and Power in an Ecuadorian Town: The Negroes of San Lorenzo.* Stanford, CA: Stanford University Press.

Whitten, Norman E., Jr. 1976. *Sacha Runa: Ethnicity and Adaptation of Ecuadorian Jungle Quichua.* Urbana: University of Illinois Press.

Whitten, Norman E., Jr. 1977. "Etnocido Ecuatoriano y Ethnogénesis Indígena: Resurgencia Amazónica ante la Colonización Andina." In *Temas Sobre la Continuidad y Adaptación Cultural Ecuatoriana,* ed. Marcelo F. Naranjo, José L. Pereira V., and Norman E. Whitten Jr., 169–213. Quito: Prensa de la Pontificia Universidad Católica.

Whitten, Norman E., Jr. 1996. "The Ecuadorian Levantamiento Indígena of 1990 and the Epitomizing Symbols of 1992: Reflections on Nationalism, Ethnic-Bloc Formation, and Racialist Ideologies." In *History, Power, and Identity: Ethnogenesis in the Americas, 1492–1992,* ed. Jonathan D. Hill, 193–217. Iowa City: University of Iowa Press.

Whitten, Norman E., Jr. 2003a. "Introduction." In *Millennial Ecuador: Critical Essays on Cultural Transformations and Social Dynamics,* ed. Norman E. Whitten Jr., 1–45. Iowa City: University of Iowa Press.

Whitten, Norman E., Jr. 2003b. "Symbolic Inversion, the Topology of *El Mestizaje,* the Spaces of *Las Razas* in Ecuador." *Journal of Latin American Anthropology* 8 (1): 52–85. https://doi.org/10.1525/jlca.2003.8.1.52.

Whitten, Norman E., Jr., and Kathleen Fine. 1981. "Introduction." In *Cultural Transformations and Ethnicity in Modern Ecuador,* ed. Norman E. Whitten Jr., 1–41. Urbana: University of Illinois Press.

Whitten, Norman E., Jr., and Diego Quiroga. 1998. "To Rescue National Dignity: Blackness as a Quality of Nationalist Creativity in Ecuador." In *Blackness in Latin*

America and the Caribbean, vol. 1: *Central America and Northern and Western South America*, ed. Norman E. Whitten Jr. and Arlene Torres, 75–99. Bloomington: Indiana University Press.

Whitten, Norman E., Jr., and Dorothea Scott Whitten. 2011. *Histories of the Present: People and Power in Ecuador*. Urbana: University of Illinois Press.

Wolf, Eric. 1955. "Types of Latin American Peasantry: A Preliminary Discussion." *American Anthropologist* 57 (3): 452–71. https://doi.org/10.1525/aa.1955.57.3.02a00050.

Wood, Robert E. 1984. "Ethnic Tourism, the State, and Cultural Change in Southeast Asia." *Annals of Tourism Research* 11 (3): 353–74. https://doi.org/10.1016/0160-7383(84)90027-6.

World Bank. n.d. Accessed June 12, 2016. http://projects.worldbank.org/P039437/poverty-reduction-local-rural-development-prolocal?lang=en.

Yashar, Deborah J. 2005. *Contesting Citizenship in Latin America: The Rise of Indigenous Movements and the Postliberal Challenge*. Cambridge: Cambridge University Press. https://doi.org/10.1017/CBO9780511790966.

Yellow Bird, Michael. 1999. "What We Want to Be Called: Indigenous Peoples' Perspectives on Racial and Ethnic Identity Labels." *American Indian Quarterly* 23 (2): 1–22.

DANIEL BAUER is an associate professor of anthropology at the University of Southern Indiana. He is conducting active research projects in coastal Ecuador and Amazonian Peru. His research focuses on development, tourism, identity, and resource use. He is also founder and project coordinator of REDI (www.ruralecuador.org). All author royalties from the sale of this book will go to support REDI projects aimed at rural development and poverty alleviation in coastal Ecuador.

Index

Ecotourism and Community Development, 122–23

Ecuador, 5, 98, 111, 122; economy in, 19–20; Indigenous movements in, 84–87, 138; mestizaje in, 83–84; migration patterns, 29–30, 54(n1); national census, 102–3

Ecuador (Meggers), 57

Ecuador Runacunapac Richarimui (ECUARUNARI; The Ecuadorian Indian Awakens), 84–85

Eduardo, 114

elites, 19, 39, 58

El Oro province, 86

Elsa, 104

El Tropical, 37

encomienda system, 82, 107(n3)

environment, and identity, 51–54

Esmeraldas, 86

essentialism, 85

Estatuto del Pueblo Manta, 104

ethnic identity, 4, 66, 68, 83, 94; self-perception of, 106–7; survey on, 102–3

ethnicity, 17, 18, 42, 84, 103, 106; politicization of, 93, 94

ethnogenesis, 17–18, 22, 94, 100, 105, 138

ethno-racial hierarchy, 10, 81, 82

Evangelical Church, 31

ex-pats, 10

Facebook, tourism, 13

family, fishing industry, 36

fantasma, 43–44, 139; cultural position of, 45–46

FEPTCE. *See* Plurinational Federation of Turismo Comunitario in Ecuador

Festival de la Balsa Manteña, 57, 66; activities of, 68–72; preparation for, 67–68

Festival of San Pedro and San Pablo, in Machalilla, 31, 32–33

festivals: ancestral ties, 66–76; Catholic, 31, 32, 33

fibras, 36, 114; four tourism, 129–30, *131*

fieldwork, 5; in Ecuador, 5, 6–14

finances, for tourism, 115–16, 117–18

fishing, 21, 48–49; from bongos, 46–47; cultural importance of, 41–42; and *fantasma*, 43–45; night, 42–43; reciprocity in, 50–51; rod and reel, 39–41; sport, 112

fishing boats, 54(n4); in fishing process, 47–49; ownership of, 36, 39

fishing industry, xiv, 21, 55(n6), 55(n7); cultural processes in, 42–43; marketing, 49–51, 87; Salango's, 30–31, 36, 38–39, 87; status in, 33–34, 35; processes in, 46–49

fish transporters, 35

food, regional, 13

Francisco, don, 31, 32–33, 39

friendship, and fieldwork, 8–14

Fundación Presley Norton, 73

Fundación Pro Pueblo, 73, 88

Galapagos Islands, 25, 29; diving in, 113–14

Gallo, don, 35

garua, 24

Gaucho, El, 133

gaveteros, 35

Germany, Ecuadorian migrants in, 29

gifting, of fisheries, 51

global connectivity, 23

gringos, 9–10, 23(n11), 88; in *fantasma* story, 44–45

Guayaquil, 29, 30, 49, 69, 87, 111; transportation from, 10–11

Guayas province, ethnic identity in, 86, 87

guide licenses, 116, 131

Gustavo, 8, 9, 31, 34

hacienda buildings, 58

hacienda system, 16, 23(n4), 37, 82–83

Hector, 67

Highway E15, 22, 87–88, 111, 138–39; protests on, 89, 91–92

huacas, 58

Huaorani, 85

Huarochirí Manuscript, The, 58

huasipungo system, 16, 23(n4)

identity, identities, xiv, 59, 66, 81, 98, 106, 139; archaeology and, 21, 22, 56–57, 99; and belonging, 140–41; community, 75–76, 93–94; and economy, 4, 41–42; environment and, 51–54; and mestizaje, 20, 79–80; mestizo, 14–15, 97; in plurinationalism and multiculturalism, 100–101; reframing, 86–87, 90–91; survey on, 101–3; tourism and, 127, 134

identity formation, politics of, 96–99

Pueblo Manta-Wankavilkas, 87, 93, 138
Puerto López, 28, 34, 72, 111, 115; police in, 7–8; tourism, 116, 117, 133, 134
pulmón, al, 38
Puyo, 16

Quito, 29, 69, 77, 111

race, 14, 79, 103, 106; flexibility of, 15–16
rafts: balsa trading, xiii, 58, 134, 145; in Festival de la Balsa Manteña, 68, 71–72
rainy season, 24, 25
Raza Cósmica, La (Vasconcelos), 14
reciprocity, and sense of community, 50–51
reducciones, 82, 107(n3)
regional connectivity, 23
regulations, tourism, 132–34
religion, in Salango, 31–32
República de los Indios, La, 82
resistance, 68, 82
resource extraction, 83
rights, 20; Indigenous, 83
Rio Bamba, Indigenous Uprising in, 77
Río Chico, 27, 123; self-identity in, 101–2
Ríos Profundos, Los (Arguedas), 83
ritual practices, rituals, 31, 57, 74; politics of identities, 16–17
roads: Indigenous Uprising occupation of, 77, 78; to Salango, 22, 87
rod and reel fishing, 39–41
Rodríguez Lara, Guillermo, 16
rowboats (*bongos*), fishing with, 38, 42, 46–48
Ruíz, Bartolomé, 99
Ruiz Navas, José Mario, 83
rural development, 125

Salango, xiii–xiv, 21, 24, 25; archaeology in, 61–64; changes in, 137–38; coastal highways and, 87–90; community-based tourism in, 121–24; as comuna, 27–28, 93–94; demography of, 29–30; economy of, 30–31, 36, 37, 38–42; as fishing villages, 13–14; Highway E15 and, 87–89; identity in, 75–76, 86; land sale protest in, 91–93; outsiders in, 138–39; region in, 31–32; self-identity in, 101–3; *Spondylus* workshops at, 59, 60; tourism in, 111–12, 114–15, 133, 143–45; transportation to, 10–11
Salango, Isla, 62, 116

Salango Lindo (song), 52–54, 103
Salinas, fishing industry and, 87
Santa Elena province, 86
Santo Domingo Cathedral (Quito), Indigenous Uprising, 77
scenic overlook (*mirador*), 122–23
sea cucumber (*pepino*), season for, 113–14
Secoya, 85
self-identification, 97, 106–7
sendero ecológico, 122
Señorita Manteña Bonita contest, 70–71
shamans, 70, 73, 74, 75
Shiwiar, 85
Shuar, 85
Siona, 85
snorkeling, 112
social differentiation, 21
social hierarchy, ethno-racial, 81
social mobility, status and, 33
social relations, reciprocity in, 51
social reproduction, 66
social status. *See* status
social stratification, hacienda system, 37
song, 103; and ocean environment, 52–54
Spain, Ecuadorian migrants in, 29
Spondylus spp., 57, 61, 70, 134, 139; artisans, 64–66; cultural importance of, 58–60
sport fishing, 112
status, display of, 32, 33–35
structural adjustment, 19
subjugation, of identity, 16
Suizo, El, 88, 89, 95
survey, on self-identity, 101–3
symbolism, *Spondylus* carvings, 65–66

tagua palm nut (*Phytelephas aequatorialis*) carving, 125
taller artesanal, 123
taxation, race and, 103
terrenos ancestrales, 26
terrenos comunales, 26
territoriality, 105–6
territory, ancestral claims, 90
Toledo, Roberto, 27–28, 76, 89, 126; community protest, 91, 92, 93
tourism, xiv, 22–23, 65, 72, 122, 143–44; bribes in, 131–32; bureaucracy, 132–34; as community development, 110–12, 120–28, 135, 145; cooperatives, 112–13, 119; divers and, 114–15;

financing, 115–16, 117–119; and identity, 135–36; licensing, 116–17; politics of, 139–40; private investment in, 129–31
tourism boats, 129–30, *131*, *132*
transportation, to Salango, 10–11, 87
tribute system, 82
turismo comunitario, 124–25; resident interpretations of, 127–28

United Nations, on indigenous identity, 97
United States, Ecuadorian migrants in, 29

Valdivia culture, 58
value, ethnic identity, 83
Vasconcelos, José, 78, 79; *La Raza Cósmica*, 14
vendors, in informal economy, 12, 13
Venezuela, Ecuadorian migrants in, 29

villages, fishing, 13–14
visitors, to Festival de la Balsa Manteña, 69
viveros, 123, *124*

wealth, 32; concentration of, 19–20
whale watching, 112, 116, 118
Whitten, Norman E., Jr., 16
Witt, Jamil Mahuad, 19
workshops, artisan, 123, 125
World Bank, 19, 20, 97, 139; tourism development, 22–23, 110, 122

Yasuni Reserve, 83
Youth Center for the Development of Salango (CEDESA), 67, 68

Zapotec, 94